D0822914

FORGIVE & LOVE AGAIN

JOHN W. NIEDER
THOMAS M. THOMPSON

HARVEST HOUSE PUBLISHERS

EUGENE, OREGON

Cover by Dugan Design Group, Bloomington, Minnesota

Cover photo © iStockphoto / andipantz

> The names of some of the people appearing in this book have been changed to protect their privacy.

FORGIVE AND LOVE AGAIN
Copyright © 1991 by John Nieder and Thomas M. Thompson
Published 2010 by Harvest House Publishers
Eugene, Oregon 97402
www.harvesthousepublishers.com

ISBN 978-0-7369-2905-9

Library of Congress Cataloging-in-Publication Data

Nieder, John.
    Forgive and love again / John Nieder, Thomas M. Thompson.
    ISBN 0-7369-1216-9
    1. Marriage—Religious aspects—Christianity. 2. Marriage—Biblical teaching. 3. Forgiveness—Religious aspects—Christianity. I. Thompson, Tom. II. Title.
BV835.N545 1991
248.8'FT44—dc20
                                       91-3313
                                       CIP

Printed in the United States of America

10 11 12 13 14 15 16 /BP-KB/ 10 9 8 7 6 5 4 3 2 1

For additional information about the ministries
of John W. Nieder or Thomas M. Thompson,
visit www.johnonline.org,
e-mail info@johnonline.org, or write to

John W. Nieder
The Art of Family Living
Box 610350
Dallas, Texas 75261

Special Thanks…

To Marcia Jean Thompson and Teri Nieder for practicing what their husbands preach. You are both great forgivers, and we are grateful.

To Rod Anderson for challenging our thinking both biblically and practically. You are a beloved brother.

To Greg Enos for his keen insights and editorial efforts. Your contribution to this book cannot be overstated.

To Lisa Allen for her servant's heart and distinctly feminine perspective. Your encouragement and graciousness helped bring this book to reality.

To the entire staff of The Art of Family Living for doing double duty while this book was being written. Your commitment to the Savior and your partnership in this effort motivated and challenged us.

To Bob Hawkins, Jr. and the entire Harvest House team. Your patience, persistence, and professionalism are deeply appreciated.

Contents

1

Hope for the Wounded Heart

*H*olly sat down at the kitchen table with a cup of coffee and a blank sheet of stationery. Brian had left for work, and the kids were off to school. She was alone. It was time to write the letter. *It will be difficult,* she reminded herself. But she knew she had to do it.

Her pen hovered over the paper for a thoughtful moment. Then at the top of the sheet she wrote, "Dear Daddy, You've been gone for almost 20 years now, and I've been angry with you almost as long."

Holly paused as the words in front of her triggered a flood of memories and feelings about her late father. She winced as she thought about his stern demeanor that prevented him from showing her any affection as a child. She again searched her memory for an incident when he hugged her or said "I love you" or "I'm proud of you." But all she could hear echoing in her mind were his painfully haunting words: "You're such an ugly child."

She remembered the time as a seven-year-old when her father, a deacon in the church, disciplined her angrily by hitting her on the back with a shovel. Then, when he finally consented to take her to the hospital, he lied to the doctor about the cause of the cuts and bruises on her back. She wondered at the time how he could tell an outright lie and call himself a man of God. She didn't understand until much later that he knew he would be arrested for child abuse if he told the truth. *It's been 25 years, and the physical scar is long gone*, she thought. *But even after all these years I can still feel the emotional scar from that experience.*

Holly fortified herself with a sip of hot coffee as she recalled how as a child she wished that her father would die, even prayed that he would die. Then, a month after her twelfth birthday, he did die. *I didn't miss you, Daddy*, she mused painfully, *but I did miss having a father*.

Holly thought about her teen years and early twenties and how she allowed herself to be used by several men, desperately hoping that she would find in them the acceptance and love her father never provided. She wondered again, for the umpteenth time, how different her life would have been if she had grown up feeling good about herself instead of wishing she was somebody else.

Holly sighed deeply. "But that's all behind me now," she reminded herself aloud. "I've been set free, Daddy, and I just need to tell you something." Holly returned her pen to the paper and wrote:

> Please know that today I let go of all my bitterness and anger toward you. I let go of the feelings of hate I've held inside me for so long. I can't grow in life and be the person God wants me to be with so much anger and resentment festering inside. I must let it go now. I forgive you.
>
> I've often wondered what happened in your life to make you so bitter, so hateful, so unaccepting, and so unloving. Surely there was a time when you were full of love for others and for God. I wish I'd known that side of you.
>
> Maybe now I'll be able to visit your grave on Memorial Day and Father's Day and really

feel a sense of loss. Up until now I've gone because it was expected of me. And the last few years I refused to go at all. I know it will take a while for my feelings to adjust to my decision to forgive you. But I've let go of the pain, and for the first time in my life I'm beginning to feel free.

Rest in peace now, Daddy. You are loved.

Healing for Inner Wounds

What do you do when your spirit has been wounded or your heart has been broken like Holly's? It could be that your father was a harsh disciplinarian who gave you the rod but not a relationship. Perhaps your husband left you for another woman. Or maybe you were offended deeply by a friend. The wound is still there. The blood is still flowing.

Is your heart filled with heaviness? Do you toss and turn at night? You can't stop thinking about what happened, and every thought is filled with frustration, despair, and incredible hurt. Is there a solution for your insomnia and a safeguard for your sanity? What must you do to be healed?

You already know there is no quick fix for the devastation that occurs when you have been mistreated. If there was a simple solution, someone would have packaged it by now and made millions. I, for one, would pay just about anything for instant relief when my soul is ravaged by the malicious deeds of another person.

So how then do you turn off the memories that sting every time you see or think about that person? How do you wipe away the flood of tears that flows from a great ocean of pain inside you?

Forgiveness is the key that unlocks the door to our peace, healing, and ability to love again. That's what

Holly discovered. An instant solution it is not. But it is the key.

This idea of forgiving someone who has hurt us can be both confusing and controversial. Although it is to be one of the distinguishing marks of a Christian, few of us understand what it means to forgive. This is tragic when you consider that, in His model prayer, Jesus Christ told us to forgive those who have trespassed against us (Matthew 6:12,14-15). The Savior directed us to ask for our daily bread and also extend to others daily doses of forgiveness. And then He warned that should we fail to do so, our own experience of God's forgiveness will be jeopardized.

Why then is forgiveness shrouded in so much mystery? Maybe it's because we have a hard time believing God would tell us to do something that seems to be both absurd and impossible.

First, from the human perspective forgiving another person seems downright dumb. You have been injured, so why shouldn't you go to the wall to collect what is owed to you? It is the way of the world, isn't it? It may well be, but it isn't God's way.

Forgiveness also seems impossible. The steel shackles of anger, bitterness, and even hatred chain us to the offense and the offender. We long for freedom, but we find nothing that can break the chains until we come to understand what God means by forgiveness.

Tough Questions

Forgiveness is the soil in which God nurtures our emotional healing and our ability to love once again. It's about time we pull back the curtain to see forgiveness the way God does. To do so we must answer some important and admittedly difficult questions. For example:

- Can I forgive someone when I don't feel like forgiving?

- Does forgiveness take time?

- Will I feel better once I extend forgiveness?

- Do I need to confront the person who harmed me?

- Does forgiveness mean I must resume a relationship with the person who caused me such heartache?

- Should I forgive someone who does not seek my forgiveness?

- How can I forgive myself for the things I have done?

- The thoughts of what happened still plague me. Can I ever get them out of my mind?

Do you have ready answers to these questions? If so, you are unusual. Most of us are in a spiritual fog when it comes to forgiveness, and if we are honest about it, we'd admit that our lives show it.

In this book we're going to deal with forgiveness in two important steps.

First, we need to clear away the fog about what forgiveness is and what it isn't. You need to understand why your emotions often resist the idea of forgiveness. You need to know just how to go about forgiving those who have wounded you. And you need to see the importance of forgiving yourself as well as forgiving others. We will cover these topics in Part One, Choosing to Forgive.

Second, we need to understand what happens after forgiveness. How do you handle the painful feelings that often don't agree with your decision to forgive? How do

you confront the person who hurt you in order to prevent him from hurting others? When and how do you
reconcile a relationship with someone who hurt you?
How are the dynamics of forgiveness applied to the
unique demands of a marriage? We will deal with these
questions in Part Two, Learning to Love Again.

Before you begin Part One, we invite you to make
some important initial decisions.

First, *trust God's Word*. Drop your preconceived ideas
about forgiveness and be open to what God has to say.
Remember: "The ways of the Lord are right; the righteous walk in them, but the rebellious stumble in them"
(Hosea 14:9). And His ways are not our ways (Isaiah
55:8-9). Don't settle for what men say about forgiveness.
This is God's domain.

Second, *allow the Holy Spirit to be your counselor*. He
will reveal to you the persons you need to forgive and
will give you the ability to follow through. "'Not by
might nor by power, but by my Spirit,' says the Lord
Almighty" (Zechariah 4:6).

Third, *expect God to do a special work in your life*. God
does not want you to live your life tied up in knots. He
wants to set you free from the prison of your personal
pain.

The Holy Spirit has a way of making us live the message we proclaim. Writing this book is no exception. Tom
Thompson, my co-worker at The Art of Family Living,
and I have had to test the truth we are about to teach in
these pages. Even though I serve as the principal writer,
Tom and I contributed equally to the content of this
book, and we have both personally traveled through the
principles we now share with you. This is not ivory-
tower theology with a lot of clichés and pious platitudes.
We know what the psalmist meant when he wrote, "The
sacrifices of God are a broken spirit; a broken and con-
trite heart, O God, you will not despise" (Psalm 51:17).

Is there anything standing between you and learning to forgive and love again? How about your feelings? You may well be experiencing inner turmoil and a great deal of anxiety as your heartache replays again and again in your mind. The offense may have occurred years ago, but you relive it with each memory.

As your emotions are stirred, don't turn back toward thoughts of "Why me?" or "I can't forgive." Quiet your heart now to hear fresh insight about forgiveness. Your healing and freedom lie just ahead. It's what God wants for you, and He will show you the way.

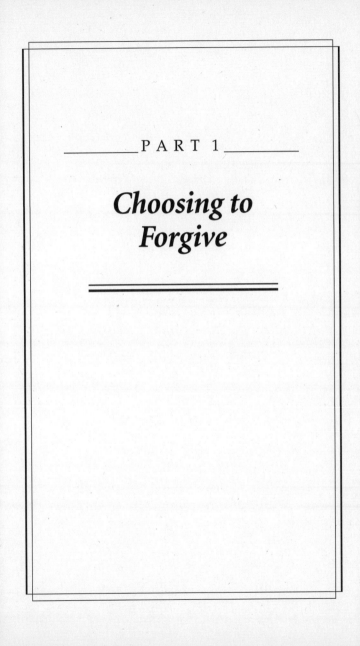

_____P A R T   1_____

Choosing to
Forgive

2

When Your Heart
Screams No

*J*oanne *was a young wife and mother who came to me
for counsel. "John, my mother is dying of cancer, and
I don't know what I should do."

"How long does she have to live?" I asked.

Joanne hesitated for just a moment. "Maybe a month."

"Is she a believer?"

"No."

"When was the last time you saw her?"

Joanne's response caught me off guard. "Almost a year ago."

It soon became evident to me that Joanne was a woman torn in two. She said she loved her mother, but she had some deep emotional scars from the past. She described her childhood as miserable. Her mother manipulated her and controlled her every move. She was embarrassed to bring friends home because she never knew what her mother would say. Now, some 30 years later, Joanne could still remember the times that her mother made her feel foolish in front of her friends. Joanne and her mother were never close, and now there was little time left.

19

I told Joanne that she had to see beyond the temporal to the eternal. My suggestion was that she write a letter to her mother expressing her love and paving the way for a personal visit. As I offered ways she could present the gospel to her dying mother, Joanne didn't seem interested. When I ended our time together and prayed for her mother's salvation, I sensed I was praying alone.

Joanne never wrote or visited her mother, who eventually died from bone cancer. Although I had never met this woman, I cried in my heart as I thought of her excruciating pain and her Christless eternity. And I thought of Joanne, who knew what she should do but didn't do it. Later she would say her heart just wouldn't let her.

Throughout her life Joanne had refused to admit her true feelings toward her mother. She was bitter and filled with hate, but she never opened up until after her mother died. It happened as she stood by her mother's open casket. Looking at the lifeless body of her mother, Joanne came face-to-face with herself and had nowhere to hide.

In counseling at a local clinic, Joanne eventually admitted that she didn't care that she never got to see her mother before she died. And then she poured out the horror story of her past, and her anger and hostility grew as her counselor listened.

In months of weekly sessions Joanne's counselor never once challenged her anger or bitterness. Joanne's emotions were merely a given. They were never questioned. She was allowed to remain angry and bitter, and never once did the counselor say that these feelings indicated that something was wrong within Joanne.

In the old days, feelings were seldom questioned in counseling. Instead they were analyzed in hopes of discovering what may have occurred in the past that caused them to bubble up through the subconscious mind. Joanne traced her feelings as well as some of her behavior patterns back to her relationship with her mother. But even after almost two years of looking back, she was still locked in emotional bondage.

What Our Emotions Reveal

If you have been emotionally wounded by a parent, spouse, child, friend, co-worker, or whomever, and you experienced some of the same emotions toward this person that Joanne felt toward her mother, don't be surprised—you're normal. God designed your heart to be sensitive to inner pain just as He designed your hand to be sensitive to a hot stove. Like the pain sensors in your hand, your inner sensitivity to hurt is an emergency warning system prompting you to do something—fast! If you didn't have these warning systems, there would be something wrong with you.

How would God have us view our emotions toward those who hurt us? Ignoring or denying how we feel about someone is not healthy, nor does it honor God. Emotions are symptoms that reveal the realities of the heart, what is really going on within us. For example, if my voice trembles with emotion when I speak, it reveals my fears and insecurities. When I cry, my tears tell me there is either overwhelming joy or deep heartache inside. Anger is the outward expression of frustration or despair within. Bitterness reveals a sour spirit or anguish that has been etched on the heart.

If we don't freely admit how we feel about others, we will fail to recognize that something may be seriously wrong at the very core of our being. Denying our emotions will never bring us to maturity in Christ. When you fail to acknowledge the offense, you will fail to forgive the offender. You cannot fully forgive what you have not fully faced.

Our emotions must then force us to examine ourselves in light of the Word of God. For example, ongoing anxiety that does not have a physical basis indicates a heart that has not fully come to know the peace that surpasses understanding (Philippians 4:7). Outbursts of anger indicate red-hot frustration and the need for the control of the Holy Spirit, who produces gentleness and self-control (Galatians 5:23). God does not want us to deny our emotions, but at the same time He does not want us to simply accept them when they are detrimental and hurtful to our relationships.

Many times forgiveness is just beyond our reach because we have not been emotionally transparent with ourselves. We are afraid to come to grips with how deeply we hurt, or we are unwilling to confront the pain in our lives. Unfortunately, until we are willing to be transparent with God and ourselves, we can block the very help we need from the Holy Spirit to forgive.

Since God made us, there can be no better source of guidance for understanding and dealing with our emotions than He. Consider Jesus Christ, who in His humanity had to deal with emotions. Having shared in our humanity, Jesus still considered certain emotions to be sinful. He said if we hold on to anger toward a brother, we are subject to His judgment. As far as He was concerned, unchecked anger was equivalent to an act of murder (Matthew 5:21-22).

Hatred is another emotion that the Savior clearly opposed. In His day those in the religious establishment thought it appropriate to harbor hate toward their enemies. In direct contrast to their beliefs, Jesus said, "Love your enemies and pray for those who persecute you" (Matthew 5:44).

Jesus made it abundantly clear that our ability to love even in the face of opposition was to be the telltale mark that we are sons of the Father in heaven. Jesus was not impressed with anyone's ability to love the people who already loved them. To do so didn't mark anything unusual in the life of an individual. But Jesus knew that His followers would be able to love even the unloving, and in so doing they would be perfect, or mature, like their Father in heaven (Matthew 5:43-48).

Before returning to heaven, Jesus once again addressed this theme. He told His disciples that the world would hate them just as it hated Him (John 15:18). But He announced to them that they would be marked by an ability to love that the world could not comprehend. They would be able to love in the face of hate. They would be known by their ability to love.

The Source of Our Emotions

Why does Jesus Christ expect us as His followers to get beyond "normal" emotions in order to love even those who harm us? Because He has given us a totally new nature with which to relate to others. He has given us the capacity to live, love, and forgive as He did.

But at the same time there remains in us a remnant of our old ways where hate and bitterness rule. There is a tendency within us that produces emotions and actions that are in direct opposition to how God wants us to live. The Bible refers to this tendency as the sin nature or the flesh. There are a number of emotions that are tied to our sin nature. Among them are hatred, jealousy, and rage (Galatians 5:20). These emotions are real and, as far as God is concerned, wrong. They are not only wrong; they are dangerous because they lead us into spiritual darkness.

The apostle John referred to himself as "the disciple whom Jesus loved" (John 13:23). It is John's closeness to the Lord Jesus Christ that makes his first epistle all the more intriguing. Mindful of what Jesus said about certain emotions such as anger and hatred, John wrote, "Whoever hates his brother is in the darkness and walks around in the darkness; he does not know where he is going, because the darkness has blinded him" (1 John 2:11).

The implication of these words is very clear. If we feel hatred toward another person, it places us in spiritual darkness, and we begin to function as if we are blind to the true spiritual realities of our world.

May I ask you a very important question? Is it possible that you are presently in spiritual darkness because you have allowed your anger to evolve into dislike or even deep hatred for a person God says you really ought to love? To answer this question you may have to consider your present spiritual condition. You may have found that your fellowship with God has not been what it used to be since you suffered at the hands of another person's actions. Such spiritual darkness is frequently accompanied by a lack of real joy and peace in your walk with God.

Are these symptoms descriptive of your present condition? If so, it may well be that you have placed yourself in darkness because you are tied up in emotional knots over an offense that has taken place in the past.

Emotional Bondage

There is another emotion closely associated with anger and hatred that is seen far too often in the lives of many believers: bitterness. Bitterness is anger stretched over time. God makes it very clear that He does not want us to be bitter toward those who have hurt us. His Word admonishes us: "Do not grieve the Holy Spirit of God, with whom you were sealed for the day of redemption. Get rid of all bitterness, rage and anger, brawling and slander, along with every form of malice" (Ephesians 4:30-31). Imagine: God is grieved when we allow certain emotions to remain in our lives! He does not want us to be bitter or filled with rage or anger.

So what do we do when we have these emotions? We get rid of them. But how? The solution is, "Be kind and compassionate to one another, *forgiving* each other, just as in Christ God forgave you" (Ephesians 4:32, emphasis added).

As far as God is concerned, we do not have to be in bondage to vengeful emotions. We can dispose of them through love and forgiveness.

Jane, a middle-aged single parent, lived a life of intense hatred for her ex-husband for years. Her anger consumed her mentally and physically. Migraine headaches eventually led to a complete nervous breakdown, after which she contemplated suicide. For years she tormented herself with the question, "How could he leave me with three young children?"

Her body continued to suffer under the weight of her fury until she realized she was about to lose everything, including her children. In desperation she met with a group of "prayer warriors" who prayed with her about forgiving her ex-husband. Afterward she wrote:

> When I went to leave my newfound friends that evening, I knew that I had the peace of Christ, the peace of forgiveness. I forgave my ex-husband, and I was instantly free. I had carried this terrible weight of hatred and guilt for almost 12 years. It was a long, hard struggle, and the solution was so obvious. Unfortunately, I could not see it, and I want to stress that I *chose* not to see it because I was feeding my anger, and it eventually became a way of life.

Looking back, Jane realized she was being consumed by her hatred. She lost her health and almost mortgaged her relationship with her own children. It was then that she was lovingly confronted with her need to forgive. And with the prayer support of some concerned Christians she forgave her ex-husband. She released him through forgiveness, and her life and health improved dramatically.

Jane broke through the emotional barrier that stood in the way of her healing. She waited 12 years to finally forgive. But when she did, the healing grace of God started to flow into her life.

Is an offense lodged in your spirit so that it has become a cancer? Does it so aggravate you that it has robbed you of your happiness or even your health? If so, then you desperately need to forgive. Don't wait and waste 12 long years as Jane did. You can begin to get rid of these negative feelings if you are willing to forgive.

Resistant Emotions

Ironically, even when we know that the answer is forgiveness, still something in our heart cries out, "I don't want to forgive him!" These feelings are not unusual. When someone plunges a dagger into our heart, we seldom respond with an overwhelming desire to extend forgiveness to the offender. Emotions such as anger and hostility immediately spring up from the old nature and clamor for revenge.

So what can we do? Our choices are limited. We can either allow ourselves to be imprisoned by these feelings, perhaps for a lifetime, or we can dispose of them as God says we should. But God's method for putting these feelings behind us is forgiveness, and forgiveness runs contrary to our natural response to being hurt. In order to forgive we must do something we don't feel like doing.

So often our motto is "If it feels good, do it." But life is filled with things we do even when we don't really feel like it. Who feels like getting out of bed on a cold winter morning? Who feels like going to the dentist? Who feels like paying the IRS? Who feels like having open-heart surgery?

Imagine a cardiologist waiting for his patient to feel like having bypass surgery. He informs his patient that the blood flow to his heart is barely enough to sustain a gerbil (as long as he is not running!) and then sends him home with the admonition, "When you feel like having your chest split open, give me a call and we'll talk about surgery."

Draw an analogy to the admittedly threatening spiritual surgery called forgiveness. Yes, there are strong emotions that scream out, "No way! I can't! I won't!" But these feelings cannot be allowed to stand in the way of the life-giving act of forgiving those who offend us.

When a woman is raped, how long will it be before she feels like forgiving her attacker? When a wife is unfaithful, how long will it take for her husband to feel like forgiving her? When a drunk driver crosses the median strip and kills your teenage daughter, when will you feel like forgiving him? When a trusted friend slanders you behind your back or betrays a confidence, when will you feel like forgiving her?

Let's be real and admit that if we wait until we feel like forgiving, it will be a long time coming or it might never happen. It may take years, even a lifetime, to settle our emotions to the point where we are "comfortable" with forgiving. There are times in life when we must do what is right even when the thought of it is distasteful. Jesus told us to love our enemies. No matter what they have done or how we feel about them, we are to respond in love to those who hurt us, valuing them as He does. He does not expect us to feel "warm fuzzies" for our enemies, but He does challenge us to do what is right, even when it runs contrary to our emotions.

Christ is our example. As bloody sweat dripped from His brow, Jesus cried out to His Father, "Take this cup from me" (Luke 22:42). The whip of the executioner was far from inviting. Jesus did not relish the thought of having nails driven into His wrists or having a crown of thorns jammed onto His brow. He didn't long to be ridiculed, mocked, and spat upon. He didn't feel like being crucified.

But the Savior refused to give in to His fear and anxiety. Contrary to the swell of His emotions that produced blood-filled sweat, our Lord did what He had to do. He said yes to the Father's will. He said yes to the cross.

For us, forgiving others is like the Via Dolorosa, the way of the cross. Our emotions create in us a crisis of the will. In the deepest part of our being, our sensitivities scream out, "No!" But God says, "Yes!" And like the One who bought our forgiveness, we must do what is right and trust the Father for the results.

It's time to agree that we cannot allow our feelings to stand in the way of what we must do. So how do we go upstream against the rapids of our emotions? By begging God to help us. We must turn to Him in our own Garden of Gethsemane and say, "Not my will, but yours be done" (Luke 22:42).

The powerful human emotions that caused Jesus to beg His Father for another way did not stop our Savior from going to the cross. And we should not allow similar emotions to stop us from forgiving one another.

Forgiveness is not something we can do alone. We don't have the power or capacity within ourselves. If we don't allow God to forgive others through us, our meager human attempts will be hollow and meaningless. We must rely on the grace of the Great Forgiver manifested through us. Who better to help us to forgive when we don't feel like it than the One who forgave the whole world?

Count the Cost

Make no mistake about it: Forgiveness will cost you something. You assume the loss. You take the hit and agree never to try to get even.

On a rafting trip down the Rio Grande River, Mike and Jamie and their guide came under fire by snipers perched on cliffs overlooking the river. Since the banks of the Rio Grande are narrow and at places impassable, they had no choice but to abandon their raft and run for cover. Mike, a huge hulk of a man, took the lead as he had done in his combat days in Vietnam. Jamie did her best to keep up. They were like trapped animals. They had become target practice for a couple of degenerates.

Jamie was clawing over the rocks when she was hit in the back. She remained conscious and made it down the river to a narrow bank. Mike was standing between the snipers and his injured wife when another shot rang out and a bullet ripped through his back. Jamie could hear the dull thud as Mike's body fell. She dragged herself under some bushes and began to cover herself with dirt for camouflage.

Mike took the bullet that was aimed for Jamie. He gave up his own life to preserve hers.

In the moments before that fatal shot rang out, Mike's fears must have challenged his love for Jamie. But he didn't allow his emotions to stand in the way of making the decision to give up his life for his wife.

Are you willing to lay aside your resisting emotions to do the right thing? I know your heart screams, "No!" You want justice. But you will have to give up your right to revenge. It will cost you. But it is the right thing to do. Forgive. With God's help you can exercise forgiveness and be healed emotionally.

Heartfelt Forgiveness

But maybe you aren't experiencing this battle between your emotions and your will. Can you still make a heartfelt decision to forgive? The answer is yes. Jesus Christ demanded that our forgiveness be real: "Forgive your brother from your heart" (Matthew 18:35). He could have simply said, "Forgive your brother." But He added the phrase, "from your heart."

What does it mean to forgive from the heart? By "heart" Jesus meant the center of your being, the core of who you are. Your mind, your will, and your emotions are all part of the forgiving moment. Jesus was saying that we cannot make the decision to forgive as long as we remain detached, uninformed, or aloof.

When we forgive, the Holy Spirit causes us to confront what happened and at the same time comprehend the command to forgive. Our mind sees the offense and the offender. As we do, our emotions may be stirred by the unpleasant memories. But our will takes control. Will I get angry again or forgive? Will I grab hold of the hurt or release it?

But what if the emotional component is missing? Can forgiveness be real, or as Jesus said, heartfelt? Yes, but make sure that you are not denying the depth of your pain or forgetting the cost of forgiveness. As long as you are honestly acknowledging the offense and sincerely counting the cost, your forgiveness can be real.

Forgiving someone is not the result of your emotional healing; it is the beginning of it. You work from forgiveness to healing, not from healing to forgiveness. So how quickly does emotional healing take place? For some people emotional freedom is immediate and complete the moment they forgive from the heart. Those who experience this spontaneous relief are typically dealing with a traumatic offense from the past.

Yet God's Word does not guarantee that you will no longer have to deal with the difficult emotions generated at the sight or thought of the person who offended you. For many people there is an emotional battle that follows the act of forgiving someone. When you meet that person, your emotions will be stirred. If you get abused again, the inner turmoil will return. Anger and bitterness will attempt to gain control once again. But this time things will be different because you and your thoughts are different. (Later in the book we will discuss how to resolve the remnants of your emotional pain.)

Our hearts yearn for the peace and joy for which forgiveness lays the foundation. The emotions that follow heartfelt forgiveness are ones of release and renewal. These are God's gifts to those who walk in the obedience of forgiveness.

So if your heart is screaming, "I won't forgive!" don't be surprised. Remember: Those initial responses are normal. But at the same time, take a good look at God's command to forgive. He never says you will feel like it. He simply says, "Do it." But in order to do it, you must be sure you know what forgiveness really is so you won't be misled by some of the common misconceptions about it.

3

Accept No Substitutes

*M*y parents separated when I was a young boy. *They had married just before my father left to* serve in the Korean war. While trying to cope with a hasty marriage and the Marines, they got the news: A baby was on the way—me, their little Johnny.

Eight years later the pressure became too great, and their marriage started to crumble. My father moved out, and my mother had to work day and night just to put food on the table. She did the best she could, but those were tough days.

I naively thought my parents' problems were all because of money. When the battle lines were drawn, unpaid bills always seemed to be the issue. I was barely nine years of age when I decided to go to the local supermarket and carry bags and push shopping carts to help pay our bills. I was willing to do anything that could get my mom and dad back together.

During those years I had no refuge from my inner pain, no place to hide. Even the neighborhood kids taunted me: "You don't have a dad!" I don't remember if they said it once or a thousand times. But each word cut me like a razor blade: "You...don't...have...a...dad!"

Out of my emotional agony I learned to fight with my fists as well as with my words. Anger owned me. The primary outlet for my pain was an explosive temper. I became an island of apparent self-sufficiency. Whenever I started to get close to someone, I immediately constructed walls for my personal protection.

Chained to my pain, I carried the hurts that had accumulated over the years into adulthood. What else can you do with open wounds? Examining them in the name of self-understanding offers little hope.

How grateful I am that God broke into my misery. I will always remember the day He taught me about forgiveness and allowed me to put the past behind me. On that day God gave me no choice but to face the years of heartache head-on. Instead of getting angry, I listened as He told me to forgive. When I finally decided to forgive, the tears flowed. I felt relieved and somehow cleansed. I had set the captive free only to discover that I was the one who had been in prison.

What took place that day was very personal, even sacred. That day I regained ownership of my past. I found freedom. The same can happen to you, no matter what your past has been.

What Forgiveness Isn't

How do you view forgiveness? In order to find and experience the freedom of forgiveness, you need to have a proper view of genuine forgiveness. And in order to see genuine forgiveness clearly, you need to identify and reject a number of misconceptions about forgiveness that are rampant in our culture, even among Christians. Here are 10 common *misconceptions* of forgiveness you need to avoid.

1. *It is better to blame than to forgive.* In her popular book *Toxic Parents*, Susan Forward presents what might

well be the prevailing attitude toward forgiveness in our culture. In the chapter entitled, "You Don't Have to Forgive," Forward discusses how we should respond to past parental abuse. She writes, "At this point you may be asking yourself, 'Isn't the first step to forgive my parents?' My answer is no....In fact, it is not necessary to forgive your parents in order to feel better about yourself and to change your life."[1]

In effect, Forward says that you and I should place the blame for our present problems on our parents. Why not? They were "toxic"—they poisoned us. So we should let them know it. Then we will feel better about ourselves and we can change our lives.

Does this approach really work? To some degree it probably does, at least temporarily. Identifying someone else as the cause of our problem is a lot easier than saying, "I have a problem." It's easier to castigate our parents than to pardon them, especially when we're looking for a scapegoat.

But Forward's philosophy runs contrary to the Word of God. Ask yourself:

- Is blaming my parents the way to honor them? (Exodus 20:12).

- Will blaming my parents help me lead them to Christ? (John 13:34-35).

- How would I feel if my children treated me as if I were "toxic" and blamed me for their problems? (Matthew 7:12).

There are a lot of Christians who are biblically off base in this matter. Somehow we have become blinded to the clear teaching of the Word of God and have accepted in its place the thoughts of mere mortals. We would do well to heed Paul's warning to the believers at Colossae: "See to it that no one takes you captive through hollow

and deceptive philosophy, which depends on human tra-
dition and the basic principles of this world rather than
on Christ" (Colossians 2:8). Deceptive ideas abound
when we consider forgiveness.

2. *It's better to deny the offense than to forgive the offender.*
When the hurt is so overwhelming, we sometimes lie to
ourselves. That's denial. It offers immediate emotional
protection in response to trauma. When we are over-
whelmed, we are tempted to disengage in order to
survive. We act as if the offense never happened. We
bury the reality and tell no one. But then, years later,
there is an uneasiness in our spirit that tells us something
is wrong.

When Sally was a young girl, she was molested by
her cousin. Many years later he confessed what he had
done and asked for her forgiveness. But Sally refused to
face the horror of what had happened. She lied to him,
saying she couldn't remember what he had done. Later
she told me that whenever her cousin's actions came to
her mind, she forced them out by concentrating on something else. For years she had refused to deal with what
happened, and she continued to live in denial.

Are there hurtful incidents in your past that the Holy
Spirit has brought to your mind? Do you try to force
them out because they threaten you? Denial is not forgiveness, and it's not healthy.

As the Lord brings the painful circumstances of your
past to mind, confront them and, in His presence and
with His power, forgive the one who inflicted your
wounds, even the wounds of sexual molestation.

Eventually Sally stopped denying what had happened and forgave her cousin. Later she wrote, "I really
believe 'The Counselor' healed me. Two weeks ago I saw
my cousin for the first time in four years. It was wonderful to see him. I was genuinely sorry when our visit

was over. The Holy Spirit was my Counselor, and the Lord healed me completely!"

With the Counselor to guide us, we can forgive rather than deny and be deceived.

3. *Forgiveness is a superspiritual game.* Ray and Craig grew up in the same city. They attended the same church and college, then went on to graduate school together. They had developed a friendly competitive relationship over the years. But when Ray began to excel, the healthy competition gave way to envy and tension between them.

A polite distance seemed to help until one day they came face-to-face and had to talk. Without so much as a casual greeting, Craig looked at Ray and said, "I want you to know that I forgive you." That was all he said. No explanation. Ray, the alleged culprit, didn't have a clue to what Craig meant. Craig had used an air of superspirituality, exhibited by his willingness to "humbly" forgive Ray, as a ploy to regain an advantage over him.

I don't suppose there is anything more nauseating to God than a pious-sounding, holier-than-thou Christian wearing a saintly smile in the name of Jesus. This modern Pharisee manipulates others by laying a guilt trip on them for some imaginary offense and impressing them with his mask of superspirituality.

That's not forgiveness; that's fraud. In fact, when we forgive someone, there is a good chance we may never even communicate with the person that we have forgiven him.

4. *Forgiveness requires us to confront the offender.* Does forgiveness demand confrontation with the one we need to forgive? Is a rebuke required? Must you first tell your parents what they did wrong in raising you before you agree to set them free? You were victimized in a violent

assault. Do you face off with your assailant and let him know that what he did was wrong before offering him a personal acquittal?

Loving confrontation may well follow forgiveness, but it is *not* required in order for us to clear the books and be at peace. After all, the offender may be dead or live a great distance from you. It doesn't matter, because forgiveness does not demand that you communicate with that person. Forgiveness, as we shall see, is primarily an issue between you and God.

5. *Forgiveness is no big deal.* Over the years, my wife, Teri, and I have counseled many couples dealing with the heartache of infertility. I remember one wife who said rather flippantly, "I have forgiven Mark for making us wait so long before we tried to have children." Mark was genuinely sorry he had allowed his career and his concern for financial security to delay having a family.

Under his leadership they had waited too long, and they both knew it.

But his wife's statement had a false ring to it. Her longing to have a child and her empty arms demanded more than a few simple words tossed toward her husband. I walked away thinking that she had not really faced the reality of the offense and consequently had *not* truly forgiven him. It was too casual, too easy.

Because forgiveness arouses emotions in us that are difficult to handle, we can act out our forgiveness half-heartedly and even become flippant with our words. In your frustration and inner turmoil you may be tempted to simply say, "Okay, I forgive him. Now leave me alone." If the exercise is shallow or frivolous, it will be void of real meaning. Don't call that forgiveness.

You can't forgive halfheartedly. You can't forgive while you are emotionally disengaged. You can't reduce forgiveness to a simple nod of the head. Casual consent won't cut it. Forgiveness *is* a big deal. You must honestly involve your heart and your mind with what happened, and then, and only then, can you truly forgive.

6. *Forgiveness endorses the offense and the offender.* "But if I forgive him, it's as if I'm saying that what he did is acceptable." No way. Forgiving the offender does not mean you endorse the offense. Just look at how God works in our lives. God never approves of sin. In fact, He hates it. But He also forgives sins.

When you extend forgiveness, you are not saying that the adultery, the slander, or the harsh words were right. Such actions are wrong—dead wrong, and things need to change. When you forgive, you let the offender off the hook, but you don't say that what happened was right.

The main reason some of us mistake forgiveness for excusing wrongdoing is that we have a warped idea about what accompanies true forgiveness. We have the mistaken notion that when we forgive someone we must never mention what happened again or we should act like it never happened. This erroneous idea opens the door for repeated episodes of drunkenness, promiscuity, physical or sexual abuse, lying, etc. Forgiveness should not be perceived as an invitation to continue the destructive behavior, especially in the case of addicted offenders.

Therefore it's essential that once we release a person through forgiveness, we speak the truth about his offense and lovingly seek to restore him (Galatians 6:1).

7. *When you truly forgive, you forget the offense.* Forgive and forget—it sounds appealing, but the reality is missing. We can forgive. But let's be very honest: In the most literal sense of the word, we can never forget what happened. Voluntary, selective amnesia would be wonderful, but our efficient minds were not designed to forget on command.

But with heartfelt forgiveness and emotional healing we can reach the point where recalling the offender or the offense no longer triggers emotional pain. In this sense, it *is* possible to forgive and forget.

Clara Barton, who founded the American Red Cross, was asked if she remembered a despicable incident in her past. Clara's response has become well-known: "No, I distinctly remember forgetting that." We too can refuse to remember the pain, and it will greatly advance our healing.

8. *Forgiveness requires immediate restoration of the relationship*. Ruth was beaten and badly bruised by her alcoholic husband. While he slept, she quickly clothed the kids and took refuge at the home of a neighbor. Should Ruth forgive her husband for his brutality? Yes. Should she immediately return home and face another beating? No.

This admittedly extreme example makes an important point. When we forgive someone, we are not required to act like everything is wonderful and step back into the same pattern of abusive behavior.

On one of our radio programs, a very articulate young woman described years of being molested by her grandfather. This courageous woman was now married, and she and her husband, as well as her parents and her grandfather, were seeing a counselor together. She felt that she had truly forgiven her grandfather, but explained that she did not feel comfortable seeing him at family gatherings. Such visits merely served to resurface the pain of her younger years. She asked if her hesitancy revealed that her forgiveness wasn't genuine.

I commended her for her honesty and assured her that forgiving her grandfather and being reconciled to him were not one and the same.

There are counselors and teachers who believe that we must resume a relationship exactly where it left off before the offense or we have failed to forgive. This doesn't make sense biblically or practically. There will be times when you need to guard your heart after you forgive someone and resolve your own emotions before you proceed with reconciliation.

Take the example of two men who worked closely together for several years. They decided to embark on a new venture and discussed the possibility of involving another young man who had previously jumped ship when things got tough. They could not agree on what should be done with this former "junior partner."

After a rather heated exchange, Paul and Barnabas dissolved their partnership over the disagreement. Paul chose Silas while Barnabas teamed up with their former partner, John Mark. Then after faithfully serving apart, Paul wanted John Mark to rejoin him. For Paul and John Mark, forgiveness and reconciliation were separated by many months or even years.

It is important to remember, however, that in many cases complete or even partial reconciliation is unnecessary or impossible. You can genuinely forgive without restoring a relationship with the person who offended you.

9. *Forgiveness is a journey of many steps.* God commands us to forgive others. He offers Himself as the model. But does genuine forgiveness take time, or does it take place at a point in time? Is it a process or a decision?

It is interesting to compare an older work by David Augsburger to his more recent views on forgiveness. In a chapter entitled "Does Forgiving Take Time?" Augsburger wrote:

> Forgive immediately!
> Forgive when the first hurt is felt!
> The man who follows Christ in life hurries to forgive.
> Quickly. Unhesitantly. Immediately!

Knowing the great value of time, he cannot afford to let it slip by in futile pain.[2]

In a recent conversation with Augsburger, he confirmed that he had changed his view of forgiveness. He now describes it as a "journey of many steps." To view forgiveness in this way may combine forgiveness with emotional healing and reconciliation.

There are people who will refuse to forgive because they believe they are not emotionally ready to release their anger, hatred, and desire for revenge. There are others who have truly forgiven but begin to doubt what they have done because their emotions conflict with their decision. When they don't immediately feel good about the other person, they wrongly conclude, "I must not have forgiven him."

This approach undermines the clear biblical command to forgive. Forgiveness and emotional healing are not the same. The emotional healing may well take time, but it all begins with the act of forgiving, a willful decision at a point in time.

10. *Forgiveness requires extensive analysis of the past.* By its very nature forgiveness involves looking back into the past. Ideally, it's the immediate past, one day at a time: "Don't let the sun go down while you are still angry" (Ephesians 4:26). But biblical forgiveness is not in the strictest sense an analysis of the past.

Much of today's counseling works from the premise that our past holds the key to solving existing problems or difficulties. In the name of self-understanding, well-meaning counselors probe the client's past to find the underlying cause of a given behavior. Often this search is conducted in the area of the subconscious mind which can hide painful memories and experiences. Many forms of counseling are designed to surface these hidden hurts, the theory being that facing the past will free us from it.

There is considerable debate over the effectiveness of such analysis. Granted, there may be some practical benefits from examining where we have been. But great caution is necessary when delving into the depths of the past. In fact, the process may be dangerous and make matters worse.

Keep in mind that forgiveness is not analysis. Analysis looks back in order to learn; forgiveness looks back in order to leave. Analysis seeks to observe; forgiveness seeks to obey. Analysis asks "why?"; forgiveness releases the "why?" and sets you free from the past.

By drawing these distinctions are we discounting any relationship between the past and the present? Of course not. A young bride may dread marital intimacy because she was molested as a little girl by her father. A man may be an angry, desperate, driven workaholic because he was raised by a hostile, demanding dad. Wounds suffered in our significant relationships can send emotional and spiritual shockwaves that can vibrate for a lifetime if we fail to deal with them in God's way. And God's way is through the sacred exercise of forgiveness.

Are we saying that analysis of the past is absolutely wrong? If we only end up making excuses for our actions and failing to take responsibility for them, yes. If we end up blaming our parents for our problems, we have failed to forgive and have forgotten the power of God to change our lives. If we come away from analysis with nothing more than labels and scapegoats, we have wasted our time, not to mention a great deal of money.

But what if analysis challenges sinful emotions and attitudes and leads to forgiveness? Then it's no longer merely analysis, it's discipleship. It's a life-changing experience because it is based on biblical truth and made possible by the Holy Spirit.

Wife, mother, and author Maureen Rank came to the place where she could no longer ignore her inner turmoil. God revealed to her that she was suffering a profound sense of loss because she had not experienced the love she longed for from her father. In her helpful book that chronicles her experience she wrote:

> You cannot forgive or forget what you have never recalled; you cannot leave a place you have never been; you cannot release what you have never held, you cannot seek healing for a wound you have not acknowledged.[3]

If looking back leads us to forgiveness, it's healthy.

Are you willing to let the Holy Spirit help you recall the wounds you have refused to acknowledge for years? Are you willing to take one last look at these wounds so you can embark on a journey toward healing?

Why not decide that you will no longer live your life shackled to the pain of your past? Commit to God and to yourself that you will do whatever it takes to put your past behind you (Philippians 3:13-14). Determine right now that you are ready to reject any hostility that still lurks in your heart. You are going to stop blaming others for what you are doing now. You are ready to forgive and embrace your healing.

There are a lot of counterfeits for true forgiveness. Don't settle for a lie. Forgiveness only opens the door to your healing when it's the real thing.

4

The Dangers of Unforgiveness

I have a problem," you say. "It's not that I can't forgive him. I just don't want to forgive him! I know God has forgiven me and the person who hurt me. So why do I have to turn around and forgive him?"

Before we define and describe genuine forgiveness, we need to discuss the problems associated with our occasional unwillingness to forgive. You have been hurt, and you're putting your foot down. You're not going to give him the satisfaction of forgiving him. Justice—that's what he needs. And since you're the one who got hurt, you feel you're the one to bring down the gavel.

Buying Trouble

Make no mistake: Forgiveness is a choice. God will never make you forgive anyone who hurt you. You can decide not to forgive if you want to. But before you do, you'd better know what you're getting yourself into. Because if you fail to forgive those who offend you, you're only hurting yourself.

Unforgiveness imprisons you in your past. What offense has scorched your spirit? Who inflicted your wounds? If you have ready answers to these questions, the offense and the offender are still very much on your mind. You know exactly when and how the knife punctured your peace. Adultery—and you know who betrayed you. A business deal turned sour—and the face of the person who ripped you off is constantly before you. An insult—and you vividly remember every word.

Or maybe the pain is more like that of a thorn, a persistent, gnawing discomfort that tells you something is wrong. Your heart is heavy. At times you're depressed, but you're not sure why. You suspect, with good reason, that there's something you need to settle and someone you need to deal with. But who is it? What happened? And what can you do about it?

As long as you fail to identify and forgive offenders and offenses, you will be shackled to your past. Unforgiveness will keep the pain alive, pick at the open sore, and keep it from healing. You will go through life feeling just as bad as you do now, or perhaps worse, with no relief in sight.

There is another alternative. You can forgive the person who hurt you and get on with your life. Forgiveness opens the prison door and sets you free from your past.

Unforgiveness breeds bitterness. Bitterness is a devastating sin that can be directly traced to the failure to forgive. You become caustic when you continually nurse the wound inflicted by another person. Malignant thoughts and harassing memories eventually distort how you look at life. Anger begins to rage and can easily get out of control. As your emotions begin to run wild, your mind may do the same. You entertain desperate ideas for revenge. Even casual conversations with others become your forum for slander, gossip, and innuendo against the offender. Your flesh, that horrible remnant of your old sin nature, has gained control.

Steve admitted that he wanted to fight back. His partner had cheated him out of a quarter of a million dollars. Steve found himself flat broke and facing bankruptcy.

Instead of forgiving his partner, Steve allowed his mind to dwell on what had happened and then developed a plan for revenge. At first he thought it was merely a fantasy to help him blow off steam. Then he realized his imagination was fueling his hostility and destroying him physically and spiritually. He realized he would lose much more than the money unless he forgave his partner, which he finally did.

God does not want us to be bitter toward those who have hurt us: "Do not grieve the Holy Spirit....Get rid of all bitterness, rage and anger, brawling and slander, along with every form of malice" (Ephesians 4:30-31). Mark it well: The Holy Spirit is distressed when we give vent to crippling emotions such as bitterness, anger, and rage. These stand in direct contrast to what He wants to produce in our lives, namely "love, joy, peace, patience, kindness, goodness, faithfulness, gentleness and self-control" (Galatians 5:22-23). The Holy Spirit's fruit is thwarted in our lives until we get rid of bitterness through forgiveness.

Unforgiveness gives Satan an open door. The unresolved anger and bitterness that accompanies a failure to forgive is a welcome mat for demonic activity: "'In your anger do not sin': Do not let the sun go down while you are still angry, and do not give the devil a foothold" (Ephesians 4:26-27).

What is a foothold? It is a point of access and involvement. It is a base of operation that allows the enemy to advance. We normally think of a demonic foothold in terms of occultic practices, ritual abuse, etc. Less apparent, yet just as real, are the malignant emotions and attitudes, spawned by unforgiveness, that invite demonic activity. Out of his vast experience working with oppressed Christians, Neil Anderson writes: "Most of the ground that Satan gains in the lives of Christians is due to unforgiveness. We are warned to forgive others so that Satan cannot take advantage of us (2 Corinthians 2:10-11)."[1]

Chuck Swindoll agrees that persistent unforgiveness offers Satan an opportunity: "For a number of years I questioned [Christians being demonized], but I am now convinced. If a 'ground of entrance' has been granted the power of darkness (such as trafficking in the occult, a continual unforgiving spirit, a habitual state of carnality, etc.), the demon(s) sees this as a green light—okay to proceed."[2]

Maybe you have given Satan a foothold because you have been unwilling to forgive. Take heart. You can evict this trespasser, this squatter who does not belong in your life. How? By doing what you should have done long ago: Forgive.

Unforgiveness hinders your fellowship with God. Jesus said, "If you forgive men when they sin against you, your heavenly Father will also forgive you. But if you do not forgive men their sins, your Father will not forgive your sins" (Matthew 6:14-15, see also Mark 11:25-26).

The forgiveness from the Father our Lord mentions here is not the initial forgiveness we receive when we personally place faith in Christ as Savior. Your standing with God depends solely upon what Christ has accomplished for you by His death on the cross. If your eternal salvation depended on any action of yours after you believed and were declared righteous by God, then you could never be sure of your salvation.

Rather, in Matthew 6 the Lord is speaking about daily items—daily bread, daily forgiveness from God for ourselves, and daily forgiveness from us to others. God's forgiveness here is that which comes repeatedly after salvation for our daily sins.

When you sin as a Christian, you are to confess your sin to the Lord (1 John 1:9). Since it is a sin *not* to forgive someone, your attitude of unforgiveness must be confessed to God as sin and forsaken or you forfeit a measure of fellowship with God. In essence, our Lord is saying, "Don't come and confess your daily sins to Me unless you understand that it is a sin for you not to forgive someone who offends you." If you refuse to forgive others, you cannot experience the daily fullness of fellowship with God.

Don't think that we earn our forgiveness and fellowship with God by forgiving others. We never earn, merit, or deserve anything from God. Rather, we cannot truly ask forgiveness if our hearts are not right with other people.

Are you at odds with God because you have refused to forgive someone? It could be that God is holding the sin of unforgiveness against you just as you are holding the offender's sin against him. So long as you act as the judge of that person, God will stand in judgment of you.

For your own sake, we urge you to confess your failure to forgive. Don't continue to pay the price for nursing a grudge. Forgive and enjoy the breadth of fellowship with God you desire.

Why Should You Forgive?

Avoiding the dangers we just discussed should be motivation enough to change your mind about not wanting to forgive. But consider also these positive reasons.

Forgiveness exercises God-pleasing faith. The Lord's disciples expressed well the fact that faith is a main ingredient of forgiveness. Jesus told His followers to forgive a repentant brother even if he sins seven times a day (Luke 17:3-4). This took the disciples' concept of forgiveness beyond anything they had experienced before, and they responded, "Increase our faith" (v. 5).

To forgive as Jesus commands requires vibrant faith. Forgiveness is a faith issue. We are to forgive and in so doing demonstrate our willingness to trust God for the results. Jesus implied that even "faith as small as a mustard seed" (v. 6) is capable of forgiving excessive offenses.

Angela, a woman who worked in our office, discovered what mustard seed faith and forgiveness can do. Steve, her husband, left her for another woman. Could there be any greater insult? Angela had prayed for him for years. He had ridiculed her beliefs, but she never thought there would be another woman.

Angela had a sweet Southern charm, and yet there were days when the agony of her separation and pending divorce was etched on her face. Her anguish was obviously intense just before Christmas after the present she sent to her husband was returned by his girlfriend with a curt note: "He's mine now. Don't send any more presents."

A few weeks after Christmas I once again sensed that Angela's heart was near the breaking point. She asked me to pray for her because she had to have a double mastectomy. I found myself asking God, "Why are You allowing this precious woman to go through all of this?"

When she returned to work following the surgery, I was amazed to see a sparkle in her eyes. She was radiant. I welcomed her back and she immediately said, "John, I must tell you what happened. Just hours before the operation, Steve came to the hospital and asked if he could stay with me until the surgery was over and I was out of danger. I had mixed emotions, but I said yes. He was there when I went into the recovery room. He even gave me a kiss. Then for several days he called to see how I was doing."

Through it all Angela was wise enough to realize that Steve would still probably go through with the divorce.

But she also had faith that God was working on his heart. Although she held little hope for their marriage, Angela was more hopeful than ever that Steve would come to a saving knowledge of Jesus Christ. And that was what mattered most to Angela.

Was Angela too loving when she sent her estranged husband that Christmas present? Did she take too much upon herself when she allowed him to be there the day of her surgery? Had she played the fool in forgiving him? What I saw was not a fool, but a woman of faith who could see beyond both her own pain and the curtain of time.

Faith clears the air. Faith gives a second chance. Faith creates expectancy. God honors faith, and faith pleases God (Hebrews 11:6). God says, "By faith, forgive—just do it."

Forgiveness is the honorable thing to do. It's in the midst of personal difficulties that the forgiving Christian shines. Such is the case with the former coach of the Dallas Cowboys, Tom Landry.

Over the years I've been a casual fan of the Cowboys, having a great deal of respect and admiration for the late Tom Landry. One of my friends was a confidant of Landry's. More than once my friend has shared incidents out of Landry's life that demonstrate the sincerity and depth of his Christian commitment. And when I was with "The Coach" he exhibited a warmth that I found refreshing in our world of pretentious celebrities.

By anyone's standards, Tom Landry had an outstanding career as a head coach in the National Football League. He brought the struggling Dallas franchise to the status of "America's Team." But then, after nearly 30 years, the team was sold and Landry was fired, all in the same day. Most of Dallas knew what was happening before Landry did. The word leaked out and the coach was confronted by a reporter before the new owner could give him his pink slip.

The way the new owner handled the situation was insensitive at best. He was so enthralled with his new toy that he discarded Landry like yesterday's newspaper. Tom Landry was treated like a second-rate coach from a semipro team.

Landry admitted that he was surprised and hurt by the abrupt firing. But he never lost his poise or threatened to get even. Many Dallas fans were ready to lynch the new owner, but Landry never added to the hysteria. There was never even a hint of vengeance in his voice, even when one reporter after another invited him to attack those who mistreated him.

When the dust settled, Tom Landry emerged bigger than life, not only because of his record as a coach but because of his character as a forgiving Christian. People rallied around him. Ballads were written about him. Dallas honored him with "Tom Landry Day," and a massive parade was held in his honor. And he was soon inducted into pro football's Hall of Fame. Tom Landry went from being known as a famous coach to a man of honor because of his forgiving heart.

Choosing to forgive does not cheapen or demean us in the eyes of God. In fact, it is noble and Christlike to forgive. On a number of occasions the opponents of Jesus Christ challenged the Savior because He told people that their sins were forgiven: "Who can forgive sins but God alone?" (Mark 2:7). Forgiveness is first the unique prerogative of God. But our God has called us to forgive just as He does.

Run through the litany of great forgivers and you will see spiritual nobility, not emotional poverty. When Joseph forgave his brothers, we see nobility. When the prophet Hosea forgave his wife of her adultery, we see nobility. When Stephen forgave his executioners, we see nobility. When Jesus Christ cried out, "Father forgive them," we see nobility. We see God.

We are at our best when we forgive. We don't demean our dignity, we enhance it.

Forgive because God says so. "But I just can't forgive him. You can give me a hundred reasons and it won't matter. It's just not in me. Even if it's a noble and honorable thing to do—I can't forgive."

"I can't forgive" is the common cry of those who have been severely hurt by the words or actions of another. For them the thought of forgiving is met with an avalanche of emotions that block the best of intentions.

Jennifer is a case in point. Her fiancé left her. The wedding was planned, the invitations were sent, and the monogrammed towels had just arrived. Then he walked out. She not only had to tell her parents, but his parents, who were as angry with him as anyone. But that didn't help Jennifer cope with the feelings of rejection.

She was humiliated to send out announcements canceling the wedding. Each of her bridesmaids wanted to know what happened, so Jennifer repeated the story over and over until it made her physically ill. She didn't know what to do. "Do I return the presents from the bridal shower? Do I reimburse the bridesmaids for their dresses?" Every day there were more and more questions, and each one reopened the wound.

When her best friend and maid of honor challenged her to forgive, Jennifer went to pieces. Her cry was loud and clear: "I can't."

Is forgiveness a matter of ability or obedience? Is it that we *can't* forgive or that we *won't* forgive?

We would never discount the fact that emotions can create a crisis of the will. We see it far too often to deny it. Yet God's Word is clear: Forgive (Matthew 6:12,14-15; 18:21-35; Ephesians 4:32; Colossians 3:13). While God is mindful of our often conflicting emotions, the Bible also demonstrates clearly that when God calls on us to do something, He will *always* give us the ability to follow through, no matter how we may feel about it.

The beauty of obeying God's instructions to forgive is many-splendored. When you obey you are involved in a transaction with Him. Your obedience shifts your focus from the offender to God. When your thought-direction is heavenward, you tend more to see the big picture. This causes your hurt from the trespass to diminish in size and intensity. You begin to develop a sensible, scriptural perspective toward the entire offense.

Forgiveness causes calmness to govern your mind. When you focus on God first, the Holy Spirit's ministry in your life is enhanced, not hindered. He brings His comfort and sanity to you. As He ministers to you, you become an instrument of peace in His hands.

"My best advice?" writes Malcolm Boyd. "Learn to practice forgiveness. The energy loss we suffer when we harbor resentment is incalculable and self-destructive. In fact it kills. Try to spend that energy instead on moving along in a creative and nurturing way. Honor the credo 'To life!'"[3]

5

The Model of True Forgiveness

*W*e find the supreme example of forgiveness in the person of Jesus Christ. Our forgiveness was His purpose for coming to earth, and God's forgiveness is the only means by which we can forgive others.

We already understand that genuine forgiveness will cost us something. Forgiveness isn't an exercise of justice in which we are guaranteed repentance, apology, and restitution from the offender. Forgiveness is an exercise of mercy. We let the offender off the hook and relinquish all rights to compensation for the physical, emotional, material, or financial wrong we suffered at his hands. No wonder our emotions scream out, "I can't forgive! It isn't fair! I'd rather die!"

Tom Thompson, my coauthor and associate at The Art of Family Living, talks about a terrifying situation that etched in his heart an unforgettable illustration of the cost of forgiveness. Tom's life-and-death experience not only illustrates what forgiveness costs us but puts it into perspective by illustrating what it cost Jesus Christ to forgive us.

Several years ago Tom had a malignant melanoma surgically removed from his left temple. Shortly after returning home from the hospital, Tom awakened early one morning to find his pillow and the bed wet with what he imagined was perspiration. But when he turned on the light, he discovered to his horror that the pillow, mattress, box springs, and even his wife's nightgown were soaked with blood—his blood! Somehow the sutures in his temple had come loose, and pints of his blood had spurted from the facial artery as he slept.

Tom awakened his wife, Marcia, and they frantically prepared to drive to the hospital emergency room. But Tom passed out and collapsed before they could get out of the house. An alerted neighbor applied pressure to the wound while Marcia dialed 911 for an ambulance.

Tom lost a life-threatening amount of blood but survived. The sutures were replaced, and after a long, slow process of recovery he is back to running 10K's again.

"I'll never forget the scene in our bedroom on that almost fatal day," Tom says. "Blood was all over the place. I remember thinking, *With all this blood outside me, how much can possibly be left inside me? How much blood-letting can my body endure?*

"More than once during those days I thought of Christ spilling His blood for me when He hung on the cross. He hung there because of my malignant condition. He bore my sin. He endured torture to the point that His body oozed blood from a number of different lacerations and punctures. Crucifixion is a bloody business.

"My bloody bed starkly pictured the terrible price Christ paid to forgive my sin. He poured out His lifeblood willingly to cancel my debt. My forgiveness cost Him everything.

"Forgiving someone is like losing blood. Something leaves you when you forgive. You cancel a moral debt that the offender could never pay. In that moment of forgiveness you place a deposit of grace and freedom in the account of the forgiven offender."

Understanding true forgiveness begins with realizing that God forgave us first (Ephesians 4:32).

Forgiveness Is...

In true forgiveness, we "release" the guilty party. In that one word we have the core of forgiveness and the basis of a definition.

> *Forgiveness is the heartfelt decision to release the person who hurt you from the obligation incurred when you were mistreated.*

Focus your thoughts on the key concepts in this definition. Forgiveness is to be heartfelt. It involves your will, intellect, and emotions. It involves your will because it is a decision. It involves your intellect because it is based on the facts of an offense. And it involves your emotions because they carry the weight of what occurred.

Forgiveness is a decision. God tells us to forgive. Forgiveness releases the offender from ever having to pay his obligation to you. When an offense is committed, there is a moral imperative that payment must be made to compensate for the wrong. This sense of justice is written into every fiber of our being. Forgiveness cancels that moral debt.

In Matthew 18:21-35, Jesus told a parable that captures the essence of what it means to forgive. A king decided to settle accounts with all his servants. Each servant was brought before the king and told what he owed. One servant owed 10,000 talents, the equivalent of millions of dollars. The servant could not pay the debt, so the king ordered that his wife and children be sold into slavery to at least offset what was owed.

The servant fell to his knees and begged for time to repay what he owed. His master responded not by simply giving him more time; he canceled the debt and set the servant free.

And now, the rest of the story. This same servant went out from that place of pardon, confronted another servant who owed him 100 denarii, the equivalent of about $20, and violently demanded to be repaid. His fellow servant dropped to his knees and begged for time to pay his debt. But the first servant refused and had him put in prison.

When the king found out what had happened, he angrily threw the unmerciful servant in jail until he could repay the 10,000 talents he owed. Jesus concludes the parable by saying simply, "This is how my heavenly Father will treat each of you unless you forgive your brother from your heart" (Matthew 18:35).

Although there are many lessons in this parable the obvious one is this: When we truly forgive we cancel an offender's debt and release him from any obligation to repay us. Forgiveness is God's way for us to deal with and discharge the offenses of others.

To help us understand forgiveness more fully, the Bible gives no less than 88 different word pictures of forgiveness. The Holy Spirit used a vast array of terms to help us grasp this divine concept. Here are just a few of them.

- To forgive is to turn the key, open the cell door, and let the prisoner walk free.

- To forgive is to write in large letters across a debt, "Nothing owed."

- To forgive is to pound the gavel in a courtroom and declare, "Not guilty!"

- To forgive is to shoot an arrow so high and so far that it can never be found again.

- To forgive is to bundle up all the garbage and trash and dispose of it, leaving the house clean and fresh.

- To forgive is to loose the moorings of a ship and release it to the open sea.

- To forgive is to grant a full pardon to a condemned criminal.

- To forgive is to relax a stranglehold on a wrestling opponent.

- To forgive is to sandblast a wall of graffiti, leaving it looking like new.

- To forgive is to smash a clay pot into a thousand pieces so it can never be pieced together again.[1]

Allow your mind to dwell on God's sketches of forgiveness. They will give you insight into what happens when you forgive. For example, imagine yourself as an archer. An arrow from an enemy has wounded you. Perhaps the arrow represents hateful words, emotional abuse, or unfaithfulness. You pull the arrow out of your flesh, but instead of aiming it at your assailant you shoot it as far away as you possibly can. That's what it means to forgive.

Or think of yourself as a banker. In your hand is a note detailing a huge debt owed to you. What debts of others does your note list? Slander? Fraud? Rape? You carefully take the note and look at it once more. But instead of putting it back in the file, you tear it into a thousand pieces. That's forgiveness.

When we forgive, we consciously, before God, cancel the debt. We discard the note. We pardon the prisoner. We release the offender.

With the definition and importance of forgiveness clear in our minds, let's get down to the nuts and bolts. Who should we forgive? When should we forgive? What should we forgive?

6

The Essentials of True Forgiveness

*A*buse comes in many forms and at the hands of many
different people. We know some of the offenders
intimately, while others are faceless, nameless strangers.
The motives of our offenders differ. Some persons fully
intend to harm us. Others act in ignorance, unaware that
their words or actions are hurtful. The responses of these
offenders also vary. Some acknowledge their wrongs,
others do not. Some will commit never to do them again,
while others plan to do them again and again no matter
what we say or do.

Who Should You Forgive?

Just who should be the recipient of the gift of forgiveness? Are we to forgive everyone who hurts us?
What if the offender doesn't admit to what he did? Do
we forgive the person who won't acknowledge his
offense? Or if someone hurts us and doesn't even know
it, should we tell him? Or should we wait for God to
somehow open his eyes?

Our forgiveness is not to be limited by the offender's
response, nor is it to be extended only to certain viola-
tors. It doesn't matter how the offender responds after

his trespass or how heinous his assault was. We are to forgive those who offend us—period.

Forgive the faceless, nameless offender. Gail and her nine-year-old daughter Angie were driving the 600 miles back to El Paso, Texas, after visiting their family in Dallas. About halfway home in the middle of the night their car broke down on a deserted stretch of highway. They were encouraged when a truck driver pulled over with the apparent desire to be a good Samaritan. But what seemed to be their hope turned into their horror as the man pulled out a gun and forced Gail and Angie into the dusty, desert terrain far off the highway. He proceeded to violate them and shoot each of them in the head at close range, leaving them for dead.

Gail feigned death until the man drove away. Then she frantically groped around until she found little Angie, who was motionless and covered with blood. Forgetting her own pain, she crawled to the highway to get help.

She waited for 30 minutes and almost lost consciousness before a car pulled over. A kind gentleman took Gail to the nearest hospital where she told police where they could find Angie. Miraculously, a helicopter rescue team found her—alive.

As Gail shared with me the terror of that night, I was intrigued by the way she referred to the man who had brutalized her and Angie. There were no hate-filled remarks or profane words, just simple references to "the man who hurt us." Gail had already forgiven this sick stranger for what he had done. Though she faced countless surgeries because of her injuries, she never demonstrated a desire for revenge or retaliation. She knew that God and the police would deal with this man, but she and Angie were going to get on with their lives.

God calls us to forgive and does not limit our forgiveness only to offenders we know. Forgiveness is to be extended to anyone and everyone who has sinned against us, even a nameless, faceless stranger who stoops to the level of the unspeakable.

Forgive the person who never says "I'm sorry." Forgiveness is also to be extended to the person who doesn't admit to being wrong. Our forgiveness of others is not contingent on their acknowledgment or admission of guilt.

This can make forgiveness difficult. It's hard to let go of an offense when the other person lives in blissful ignorance that we have been maligned or, worse yet, just doesn't care that he has hurt us. If he would just get on his knees and grovel in the mud and beg, maybe we could and would forgive. But forgive without a confession? That's tough to do.

But think again about the implications of waiting for repentance. As we have seen, every moment we live in unforgiveness we are at odds with ourselves and God. We are chained to the painful past. Bitterness grows within us. We open the door for the devil. And we impair our fellowship with God. What if he never says, "I'm sorry; I was wrong"? Should Gail and Angie have waited for their assailant to come forward and repent before they granted him a personal pardon? No. Forgiveness is our response before God no matter what the offender's response is before us.

Many people, including some prominent Christian teachers, assume from the following passage that we should not forgive until the offending person repents: "If your brother sins, rebuke him, and if he repents, forgive him. If he sins against you seven times in a day, and seven times comes back to you and says, 'I repent,' forgive him" (Luke 17:3-4).

In the context of this command, our Lord is preparing us for offenses that will inevitably come. He admonishes us to make positive, loving, forgiving responses to anyone who hurts us. He is making a general statement about forgiveness that should not be pressed too far on the one word "repent."

Furthermore, in the Greek text the "if" in the phrase "if he repents" means "maybe he will, maybe he won't." The point of the verse is not the offender's repentance but our readiness to forgive, even if the offense is repeated an infinite number of times by the same person. In essence Jesus is saying, "You are to forgive everyone who offends you no matter how often they may do so. If they repent of their misdeeds, wonderful. But if they don't, you are to forgive just the same."

Notice also that Jesus instructs us to rebuke those who offend us (v. 3). Rebuke is a vital element in our loving endeavor to help the offender stop hurting people. But, as important as it is, rebuke is not to precede or replace forgiveness. It is a follow-up to forgiveness that should take place in certain cases. We will discuss the details of loving confrontation in chapters 12–13.

The fact that the parable of the prodigal son (Luke 15:11-32) precedes Christ's instructions about forgiveness in Luke 17 should not go unnoticed. The father's lavish welcome and restoration of his wayward son proves that he had already forgiven him before his son repented. The father had a forgiving, "welcome home" spirit in his heart when he saw his son a great distance away, even before he knew if his son was coming to repent or to demand more money. It didn't matter whether his son was a penitent or a panhandler; he was forgiven.

Forgiveness is an important aspect of love. In Paul's letter to Corinth he describes what love does and does not do (1 Corinthians 13:4-8). One thing love doesn't do is keep a record of wrongs suffered (v. 5), which is an apt description of forgiveness. The record is eliminated by forgiveness.

Jesus told us how far we are to extend love when He said, "Love your enemies and pray for those who persecute you" (Matthew 5:44). Should we expect an enemy to admit guilt or apologize for an offense before we forgive him? Hardly. But we are still commanded to love, and love includes forgiveness.

Have you been withholding forgiveness, waiting for your wayward friend to apologize? How long has it been? How much longer will you wait? Every day you wait you are chained to the offense. You have suffered enough. The offender doesn't hold the key to your freedom, you do. And the key is forgiveness.

When Should You Forgive?

Your typical day is filled with at least several minor offenses. A husband wakes up feeling miserable after a restless night and leaves for work without saying a word. No good-bye kiss, no hug, not even a "see you later." Then it's his turn to be offended. As he pulls onto the highway, another disgruntled insomniac, also late for work, cuts him off, causing a fender-bender. When he finally arrives at the office he finds that his designated parking place has been taken.

Life is filled with such frustrations. They harass us, but normally they don't devastate us.

Then there are the major affronts and assaults that tend to cripple us inside. A weary, disagreeable husband is a lot different than the husband who files for divorce. Surviving the drive to the office is one thing; getting fired when you arrive is another.

So with these minor sparks and sometimes major explosions happening around us every day, when do we respond to God's command to forgive?

Forgive immediately. Forgiveness should be the lifestyle of the believer. The daily sparks and bomb blasts of hurtful behavior should be dowsed by an outpouring of love. As 1 Peter 4:8 says, "Above all, love each other deeply, because love covers over a multitude of sins." Love as expressed through forgiveness covers many offenses.

When your husband leaves his clothes draped over the bed rail again, you shouldn't allow this aggravation to become an issue. Cover it with love and buy him the most recent edition of *Household Hints for Harried Husbands.* When your wife fails to record a check in the checkbook again, you may get exasperated, but it shouldn't ruin your life or threaten your marriage. Forgive her. When you're driving down the street and a young renegade in a hot sports car cuts in front of you to impress his woman, your temper might flair as you are paralyzed with fear. But forgive the guy and forget about pursuing him.

If we adopt a forgiving lifestyle we will allow a great many hurts to slide off us like water off a duck's back. Sure, we may feel the sting of the offense for a moment, but we just don't let it stick. We might whisper a brief prayer like, "Lord, help me respond in love." We refuse to harbor a grudge or look for a way to strike back. The offense happened, we forgive, and it's over and done with.

Remember: Forgiveness is not a process or journey of many steps. The manner in which the commands to forgive are stated in Scripture stresses that forgiveness occurs in a point of time. Also, from that point in time there are continuing positive results. Forgive immediately and the results will follow. Obedience to God is the key.

Delayed forgiveness on your part means delayed forgiveness on God's part. You cannot say, "Time will do the healing." How much time? How long are you willing to wait before your close fellowship with God, broken by your sin of unforgiveness, is restored? You will develop a forgiving spirit, not by lengthy processes of forgiveness, but by many and varied episodes of immediate forgiveness.

When you forgive from your heart immediately before God, you are doing well:

- You follow God's lead. He forgave you immediately.

- You place the matter in God's hands, agreeing with Him that any vengeance is to be His, not yours.

- You rule out procrastination and emotional paralysis.

- You do not allow yourself to develop negative, sinful habitual responses which can become character patterns.

- You forsake any time slot for the build-up of bitterness. Bitterness will gradually destroy you from within and keep you from living a full and victorious Christian life.

- You have the freedom to meet the offender. You don't need to scheme to avoid him.

- You open the door to reconciliation with the offender. You lance the boil so that healing can begin to take place.

Forgive as the Spirit reveals. In 1981, then President Ronald Reagan was shot by 25-year-old John Hinckley. As Reagan walked out of a Washington D.C. Hilton and waved to the crowd, shots rang out. A secret service agent shoved the president into his limousine while police and secret service agents swarmed around the disturbed young man.

At first the president didn't know he had been shot. Lying across the backseat of his limousine, he touched the stinging pain in his side and felt a gush of blood. Only then did he realize he had been hit and his life was in danger. Minutes later surgeons removed the 22-caliber bullet that just missed his heart.

There are times when we may take a "bullet" without being aware of it. Injurious relational bullets can remain buried in our hearts from childhood. We were innocent, naive, but we got hurt—molested, abused, or ignored. In our confusion and fear we dared not share the problem with anyone. Silence, denial, and time have conspired to bring some relief, but there is still that nagging sense that there is something wrong.

The Holy Spirit may want to perform spiritual surgery with the sharp scalpel of forgiveness. Infection has set in; no doubt the surgery is needed. There are certain bullets that must be removed if you are ever going to be healed completely. The Spirit knows exactly where the bullets are lodged and which ones need to be removed. Will you allow Him to be the Surgeon of your soul?

When should you forgive? As soon as possible. The Surgeon is ready.

Forgive when the offender repents. You'll remember that Jesus said, "If [your brother] repents, forgive him" (Luke 17:3). The admonition is clear. If God works on the heart of the person who injured you and he seeks your forgiveness, give it to him. Ideally you have already forgiven him before God, so when he asks for your forgiveness you are simply expressing verbally what is already in your heart.

Remember: Scripture does not teach that we should withhold forgiveness until a person repents. Forgiveness is not contingent on repentance; we are to forgive those who offend us whether they repent or not. But assurance of forgiveness should always be extended when the offender says, "I'm sorry. Will you forgive me?"

What Should You Forgive?

Drunk again. Another episode and another heartache.

Infidelity, the ultimate breech of security. Intimacy is shattered. Can the unfaithfulness ever be put to rest? Can the marriage be repaired?

Certain sins are so devastating that they seem impossible to forgive. Adultery, sexual abuse, divorce, murder, and slander are obvious examples. They carry with them an emotional holocaust that wreaks havoc with our desire to live biblically. Our anguish makes forgiveness appear to be impossible.

Repeated offenses also challenge our willingness to forgive. After years of alcoholism and many episodes of drunkenness by a loved one, all it takes is one more of his binges to move us to the edge of unforgiveness. Are we supposed to forgive even these kinds of offenses?

Forgive again and again. "But I am exhausted, tired, fed up with it all. Do I have to keep on forgiving? At some point, don't I lower the boom?"

You are asking the same question Peter posed to the Savior: "Lord, how many times shall I forgive my brother when he sins against me? Up to seven times?" (Matthew 18:21). Peter was being gracious. The rabbis of his day taught that a trespasser should be forgiven three times, but if he offended you a fourth time, let him have it—with both barrels.

Jesus gave a different response: "I tell you, not seven times, but seventy-seven times" (v. 22). It's obvious that Jesus was not saying, "Hold your temper for 77 offenses, then let it rip on offense number 78." His intent was to lift the lid on the issue of forgiveness, even for sins that are repeated over and over again. No matter how many times the sin occurs or how bad the sin is, Jesus told us to forgive freely, just as we have been forgiven.

Forgive even the worst offense. When someone injures us or our property, they owe us. They are responsible for their actions. If the neighbor's son rips a home run through my window, the boy and his parents are responsible to cover the cost of replacing it. The driver who runs a red light and sends your car to the junkyard owes you for repairs or a replacement. That's the law.

While windows and cars can be replaced by people who damage them, what do you do when the offense is adultery, verbal abuse, or slander? Is there some way to repair the damage done by unfaithfulness? Is there something the offender can do or say to make it right? Not really. You were molested by your father. If he decides to be a kind and considerate grandfather to your children, will that be enough to pay the debt? Of course not.

To get a proper perspective on the sin committed against us, you need look no further than the parable of forgiveness in Matthew 18. The key here is the comparison Jesus made between what we have been forgiven and what we are called on to forgive. We are like the first servant who had a huge debt—in monetary terms, millions. God has forgiven our sin, an incredible debt we could never pay.

Now we turn to others who owe us for their sinful behavior, and we discover the debt is relatively small in comparison, no matter what that offense happens to be. When we have been forgiven of a $10 million debt, should we flinch for a second at forgiving someone who owes us a paltry $20?

When we consider the severity of the harm inflicted on us, no matter how great it may seem in human terms, we must always see it next to the debt God forgave when we placed our trust in the Savior.

What then do we forgive? We forgive the debt, the obligation, that which is owed to us because of the transgression against us. We forgive slanderous accusations that have robbed us of our reputation. We forgive cutting words that have stolen our dignity. We forgive unfaithfulness that has swindled us out of our security. We forgive the actions and we forgive the person who committed the trespass.

As painful as these offenses may be, they are small change in comparison to what God has forgiven in us. Will you forgive the $20 debt of adultery? Will you cancel the $20 debt of divorce? Will you erase the $20 debt of verbal abuse? Will you release the $20 debt of slander? When you truly realize that God has forgiven the multimillion dollar debt you owe Him, you can forgive anything.

There's one more vital question about forgiveness that must be answered. We know what forgiveness is, why we should forgive, who to forgive, when to forgive, and what to forgive. We're convinced that forgiveness is essential to healthy relationships with God and others. But where does it happen? How do we do it? Where do we go to forgive?

7

Where Do You Go to Forgive?

Your husband stomped out of the house this morning without saying a word. You know his job pressures are grinding on him, but you were sitting across the table from him and he didn't even acknowledge your existence—and it hurt.

You know you should forgive him, and you're willing to do so. But what should you do? Should you call him at the office and say, "I forgive you for slashing me with your silence this morning"? Should you wait until he gets home to tell him? Where do you go to forgive?

Perhaps the offense was at the hands of your one-time fiancé. From the day you met your relationship seemed destined for marriage. All those years of waiting and praying and waiting and praying, and finally he came along. Your friends touted you as the perfect couple. And he was a Christian! Maybe that's why you dropped your guard and did what you promised yourself you would never do until you were married. You felt so secure in his love that you gave yourself to him.

But the wedding never happened. He left. One night, with little warning, he said it was over. He said goodbye. Your tears didn't matter. You stood there in disbelief and shock as he walked out the door. You felt used, cheated, abandoned.

The Holy Spirit has brought the incident to your mind and urged you to forgive. But he walked out years ago. He could be anywhere in the world; you have no idea where he is. Do you have to find him, face off, and say "I forgive you" to be healed? Where do you go to forgive?

Or maybe your father mistreated you for years, and the pain today is just as real as it was when it was actually happening. What are you going to do—especially now that he's dead? Will he continue to ruin your life from his grave? If you allow him to, he can. But since you can't go to him to tell him you forgive him, what can you do? Where do you go to forgive?

Forgive in Front of the One Who Has Forgiven You

The place you go to forgive is not to the person who has offended you. First of all, that person may be only a distant memory in your past. You wouldn't know where to find him if your life depended on it. Second, the offender may be dead. Obviously, you can't go to him to forgive. If God required you to forgive these offenders by confronting them face-to-face (which He doesn't), you'd be in deep trouble.

What about the person who is alive and near at hand—your spouse, your child, your parent, a friend? If you go to that person out of the blue and say, "I forgive you," you may lay a tremendous guilt trip on him, especially if he isn't aware of his offense. It's not your job to convict people of sin; that's God's job. So you don't go to that person to forgive, although you may go to him later in loving confrontation of his offensive behavior (see chapters 12–13).

Where then do you go to forgive? There are well-meaning counselors who recommend that you sit across from an empty chair and let that chair represent the person who hurt you. Then you proceed to speak words of forgiveness toward the chair. This may be a helpful technique, but it misses a critical spiritual dimension for the believer.

For the Christian, forgiving someone is a sacred act done before God in response to His forgiveness of us and His command to forgive others. It is a Godward act in which we trust Him to deal with the offender and bring healing to our hearts.

While traveling from Ephesus to Macedonia, Paul wrote a letter to the church at Corinth. He gave them counsel on how to handle a situation which involved formal church discipline. Apparently a man had been punished and then repented. It was time to restore him and move on.

Paul entered into this case of discipline with them. Then he makes a fascinating statement: "If you forgive anyone, I also forgive him. And what I have forgiven— if there was anything to forgive—I have forgiven in the sight of Christ" (2 Corinthians 2:10). Although Paul was miles away, he extended forgiveness to this man by expressing it to Jesus Christ. He agreed with the church's decision and communicated his agreement before the Lord.

Don't miss the significance of the phrase "in the sight of Christ." When we forgive, we talk to God, not to an empty chair. We go to God to forgive for several important reasons.

God was there when you were hurt. Whatever happened, whenever it happened, and wherever it happened, God was there. He saw your father hit you. He witnessed the assault. He heard the allegations. He was there, and in His unsearchable wisdom He allowed it to happen to you. And when you were offended, He was offended.

David expresses this truth in his touching psalm of repentance for his adultery with Bathsheba and the murder of her husband, Uriah: "Against you, you only, have I sinned and done what is evil in your sight, so that you are proved right when you speak and justified when you judge" (Psalm 51:4). God was there when David was in the bedroom with Bathsheba. He was there when David plotted Uriah's death. He saw and heard everything. David's sin against Bathsheba and Uriah was a sin against God.

When someone sins against us they also sin against God. When you sense the Holy Spirit prompting you to forgive, but it seems impossible to let go of your bitterness and pain over such a vicious act, remember that it hurts God so much more. Yet God was anxious to forgive us at a price you could not endure or even imagine: the price of His Son's death. You can go to Him because He understands the offense and the cost of forgiveness like no one else.

After delivering a message at a conference, I was being escorted through the crowd when a desperate woman grabbed my arm. With tears in her eyes, she asked me if we could talk. Although surrounded by people, she proceeded to tell me of how she had been abandoned by her parents.

I asked her what the Lord had communicated to her about their sin against her. She responded with a blank stare and started to stammer. She then admitted that she had never really taken this to the Lord. She had not sought His counsel and direction. She was willing to share this very private hurt with me, a stranger, in public, but she had never opened her heart to her God about the offense.

When you forgive, go to your Eyewitness. God was there.

God cares and responds. Even when it seems that no one cares, God does, and He promises to respond on your behalf. The apostle Paul discovered this time and again. He was beaten, battered, and even abandoned by his friends. His life and ministry were filled with heartache. Fortunately, Paul knew where to turn to forgive: "At my first defense, no one came to my support, but everyone deserted me. May it not be held against them. But the Lord stood at my side and gave me strength" (2 Timothy 4:16-17).

What an example of forgiveness! In the heat of battle, Paul's colleagues left him to fight alone. How did he do it? Verse 17 gives us a clue: "But the Lord stood at my side and gave me strength." Paul's friends left; the Lord didn't. They didn't care; the Lord did. Paul turned to the Lord and forgave those who jumped ship. He released them and experienced God's personal presence and enabling power. God cares about your hurt more than you can ever imagine. Out of His great love for you He tells you to forgive in His presence and promises to stand by your side. His Word assures you that He is well aware of the harm you suffered and that justice will be carried out. He wants you to leave it in His hands.

God will judge the offender. When we are hurt by someone else, God views it as a three-way transaction. The one who inflicted the pain on us owes us, but he must also answer to God, who acts as our personal witness and judge. Similarly, God says He wants us to respond to Him rather than to the offender and that our response is to be one of forgiveness. So when we communicate forgiveness before God, the person no longer owes us, but he still owes God. When we forgive another we trust God to act as judge and jury over the offender.

"When did you become God?" When I was younger I often used this question in response to someone who was critical of me. In our fallen humanity we seem to enjoy casting doubt on each other's motives and questioning each other's lifestyles. This tendency to condemn others runs contrary to the very essence of forgiveness. When we claim the right to judge, it often causes us to fail to forgive others. We end up taking matters into our own hands.

Paul's response to the criticism he received teaches us a crucial lesson. He said he didn't care who judged him, whether it was an individual or a court of law. The reason? God is the only One who has the authority and the capability to truly judge us (1 Corinthians 4:3-5).

Paul knew that God is our judge. God knows our motives better than we do. A day is coming when each of us will pass in review before God. This is what Paul had in mind in 2 Corinthians 5:10: "For we must all appear before the judgment seat of Christ, that each one may receive what is due him for the things done while in the body, whether good or bad."

When we refuse to forgive we judge others and assume the role that God has reserved for Himself alone. He knows what happened. He knows the motivating factors. He knows the person's heart.

It may be that the one who hurt you is as wrong as wrong can be. God's command is clear: "Do not take revenge, my friends, but leave room for God's wrath, for it is written: 'It is mine to avenge; I will repay,' says the Lord" (Romans 12:19). Retaliation is not a valid option. We are not to fight back. We should not return evil for evil. Instead we are to forgive and leave judgment to God. When we forgive we do so before God as an act of obedience and an expression of our trust in Him as judge.

God will bring good out of what happened. So often we casually quote Romans 8:28: "And we know that in all things God works for the good of those who love him, who have been called according to his purpose." Can we apply this passage to our lives when someone maligns us? Can God bring good out of a rotten divorce or an episode of infidelity? Does He really mean *all* things? Absolutely.

Young Joseph's hate-filled brothers tossed him into a pit, then sold him into slavery (Genesis 37). Was God watching? Did God care about Joseph? Could God bring anything good out of what his brothers did to him? Yes. The rest of the story chronicles Joseph's rise from slavery to become second in command in Egypt. And he was eventually reunited with his brothers and father (Genesis 39–47).

But after Jacob died, Joseph's brothers weren't sure if Joseph had really forgiven them or if he was just waiting until their father died to get revenge. They said among themselves, "What if Joseph holds a grudge against us and pays us back for all the wrongs we did to him?" (Genesis 50:15).

But Joseph's response proved that he had long since forgiven his brothers: "Don't be afraid. Am I in the place of God? You intended to harm me, but God intended it for good" (vv. 19-20). Joseph refused to stand in judgment of his brothers because he knew that this was the unique prerogative of God. His story beautifully reveals how God can bring good things out of bad experiences.

From start to finish, God is not only watching but He is working to bring good out of your personal pain and heartache. He is committed to turning it all around if you will just forgive and allow Him to do His perfect work. When we go before God to forgive, we are saying, "Lord, I trust You to bring good out of my grief and something productive out of my pain."

God reveals the need to forgive. Those of us who give our lives to the ministry of God's Word soon discover that we either learn to forgive or lose our spiritual sanity. The ministry is rewarding but also very painful. One of the biggest problems is a lack of loyalty. I have been knifed in the back more times than I care to remember.

On one occasion a young man—I'll call him Ben—waited until I left town to attack me. When I returned Ben refused to answer my repeated phone calls to make matters right. He avoided me and my invitations to get together with everyone involved. But at the same time he sought out anyone who would listen to his grievances. Ben talked to everyone else, but he wouldn't talk to me.

A close friend who knew the situation firsthand told me, "It's not worth the effort, John. Just forget about Ben and move on." So I did, or I thought I had until one day Ben's name was mentioned, and I found myself wanting to do to him what he had done to me: gossip, slander.

At that precise moment I sensed the Holy Spirit saying to me, "You haven't forgiven Ben, have you?" My desire to retaliate revealed my unforgiving heart. I confessed to God that I had not forgiven Ben for what he had done to me and my family. Forgiveness was the only way, and I knew it. I forgave him before God from my heart.

Just a few days later I saw Ben for the first time. I was totally at peace shaking his hand and inviting him to call so we could get together. He never called, but I did what God wanted me to do. It is no longer my concern. The matter rests between Ben and God.

As rocks pelted his body and his life ebbed away, Stephen gazed into heaven and saw Jesus Christ standing at the right hand of the Father. He cried out, "Lord, do not hold this sin against them" (Acts 7:60). Beaten, bruised, and bloodied, Stephen went to God and forgave those who were taking his life. Stephen knew what it meant to forgive in God's presence.

Forgiving someone is a deeply personal and spiritual expression that God directs through His Word and the Holy Spirit. When we forgive, we go before Him. He shows us who we need to forgive, and then He gives us His power to forgive.

You don't need to come before the offender or sit across from an empty chair to forgive. All you need is a willing spirit that is ready to go into God's presence and say by faith, "Lord, I forgive Mom. I forgive Dad. I forgive my spouse. I forgive my friend. I forgive before You." Are you ready?

The Sacred Moment of Forgiveness

Forgiveness is the foundation of God's relationship with us. His love, His kindness, His guidance, His protection, His mercy, His joy, His justification, His adoption of us as His children, His activity of making us holy—they all come to us through the funnel of His forgiveness. Apart from His forgiveness we would never know these spiritual blessings. The moment you received God's forgiveness was a sacred moment.

God's Word repeatedly tells us that we can and must forgive those who wrong us in just the same way that God has forgiven us. There is nothing casual or flippant about forgiveness. Just as God's forgiveness of us is sacred, the moments we spend before God forgiving others are sacred moments.

Isn't it time for you to enter into the sanctuary of God's presence for sacred moments of forgiveness? Are your hands full? Good. Bring your burdens with you, but be prepared to set them down. You have finally come to the right place to meet with the right Person about your hurts. You are carrying nothing He hasn't already seen. There are no surprises to Him.

Allow the following steps to guide you in your sacred moment of forgiveness.

Get alone with the Lord. Find a quiet place where you will not be interrupted. Take a long walk, or find a secluded place. Make this a holy experience alone with your God. Eliminate distractions so you can clearly hear from heaven. Give yourself plenty of time and space.

You may want to begin by getting on your knees. Get ready to give everything to Him, every contemptible offense and cutting word. Just tell Him, "Lord, I admit that I am a sinner just like those who have offended me. Thank You for forgiving my sins. I want to share in Your forgiving character. I want to know Your forgiving heart."

Remember that He has forgiven you. Take a moment to look back to the cross. Remember Jesus Christ with nails in His hands and feet and a crown of thorns on His head. Think about the blood that was shed to cover your sins. Think about the debt you owed to God that was paid at Calvary. Thank Him for paying such an incredible price. Thank the Father for forgiving you. You might pray something like this: "Father in heaven, Your Son had to die so I could be forgiven. And You have forgiven all of my sins against You. I have hurt You in so many ways, yet You have forgiven me. Father, please help me extend to others the same forgiveness You have so freely given me. In Jesus' name I pray. Amen."

Ask the Holy Spirit to be your Counselor. Ask the Holy Spirit, the Counselor, to show you who you need to forgive. You may be surprised at who the Lord brings to your mind. It may be a person or incident that you have blocked out for years because of the magnitude of the pain. If you experience a great deal of trauma over this event, you may need a spiritually sensitive counselor to pray with you and to encourage you from God's Word as you deal with the hurts from the past.

Write each of the names and offenses that God brings to your mind on a separate sheet of paper. Keep writing as long as the Holy Spirit keeps bringing people and hurts to mind. He wants you to clean house with His able assistance.

Don't run from the pain; release it. Take a few moments to allow yourself to deal honestly with the emotional pain you experience as you remember and write. Forgiveness is a decision, but it's not a cold, hard decision devoid of feeling. In fact, honest feelings may be the best indication that the decision is real.

As the Holy Spirit brings someone to your mind, you may relive the painful experience simply by remembering it. Instead of burying the pain or reacting against it with bitterness or anger, surrender it, release it before God.

Take each person and offense before the Lord. Pray, "Lord, before You today I forgive *(the offender)* for *(the offense).* I will not fight back or seek revenge. I am trusting You to act on my behalf. Heal my broken heart."

Destroy the record of wrongs done. Corrie ten Boom, the extraordinary Dutch Christian who was imprisoned for hiding Jews from the Nazis during World War II, discovered in a remarkable incident that she had not fully forgiven a wrong until she stopped holding on to it and cherishing her memory of it:

> I recall the time…when some Christian friends whom I loved and trusted did something which hurt me.…Many years later, after I had passed my eightieth birthday, an American friend came to visit me in Holland. As we sat in my little apartment in Baarn he asked me about those people from long ago who had taken advantage of me.
>
> "It is nothing," I said a little smugly. "It is all forgiven."

"By you, yes," he said. "But what about them? Have they accepted your forgiveness?"

"They say there is nothing to forgive! They deny it ever happened. No matter what they say, though, I can prove they were wrong." I went eagerly to my desk. "See, I have it in black and white! I saved all their letters and I can show you where. . ."

"Corrie!" My friend slipped his arm through mine and gently closed the drawer. "Aren't you the one whose sins are at the bottom of the sea? Yet are the sins of your friends etched in black and white?"

For an astonishing moment I could not find my voice. "Lord Jesus," I whispered at last, "who takes all my sins away, forgive me for preserving all these years the evidence against others! Give me grace to burn all the blacks and whites as a sweet-smelling sacrifice to your glory."

I did not go to sleep that night until I had gone through my desk and pulled out those letters—curling now with age—and fed them all into my little coal-burning grate. As the flames leaped and glowed, so did my heart. "Forgive us our trespasses," Jesus taught us to pray, "as we forgive those who trespass against us." In the ashes of those letters I was seeing yet another facet of His mercy.[1]

Just as Corrie ten Boom burned those incriminating letters she had treasured and kept within a moment's reach for so long, you must stop cultivating and nurturing your memory of the wrong you have suffered. Of course, you will always remember what happened; our memories cannot be erased like a videotape. But with the Lord's help you can refuse to keep tabs on the painful memory and the emotions that it awakens.

Love does not keep a record of wrongs done (1 Corinthians 13:5). After you have listed and prayed about a particular person and the hurts he caused you, destroy that sheet of paper to symbolize and finalize your decision to release the offender from the moral obligation incurred by his actions. You have canceled the debt. You have agreed to accept the consequences of that person's actions. You will not retaliate or seek to do that person any harm.

As you work through these steps of forgiveness, your experience may well match that of Doris, a woman who recently shared with us how God enabled her to forgive in very difficult circumstances. She wrote what happened as she and her best friend walked through a park and around a beautiful little lake.

> The sun was shining brightly, the birds were chirping, and carefree people surrounded me as they enjoyed this gorgeous spring day. But I could not share any of their feelings. I was caught in a turmoil of emotions ranging from anger and bitterness to deep pain and sadness. I angrily stomped along, kicking pebbles out of my way, barely able to carry on our conversation. I was dealing with my husband's adultery—for the second time.
>
> The first time I quietly suffered through the hurt and quickly forgave him. I hurt immensely, but with the counsel, support, and prayers of my friend, I endured. I remember the Lord whispering to me at that time, "Seventy times seven!"—showing me His command to forgive, just as Jesus had instructed Peter. The Lord also led me to 2 Corinthians 2:7: "You ought to forgive and comfort him, so that he will not be overwhelmed by excessive sorrow."

But this time was different. I was livid with anger. How could my husband do this to me again? How could he put me through this after I forgave him so graciously? What a fool I was! And then my emotions led me further into the past. Why me? Why did it *always* seem to be me who suffered? I remembered how my father died while I was still very young, and my mother became an alcoholic. I suffered through those feelings of aloneness and rejection, too. Why always me?

As I allowed my bitter thoughts and feelings to pour forth to my friend, I was also able to listen to myself. That's all I heard—myself. I was completely focused on me. But I didn't care; I was entitled to it; I was tired of being the victim.

And then, ever so gently and quietly, the Holy Spirit spoke. So this is how Jesus must have felt. He didn't do anything wrong, yet He suffered horribly. First Peter 2:22,24 states, "He committed no sin, and no deceit was found in his mouth....He himself bore our sins in his body on the tree, so that we might die to sins and live for righteousness."

Suddenly, I felt some small measure of purpose in what I was going through. "So this is how Jesus must have felt—and even more." I thanked the Lord for that insight. I was humbled at the contrast between my own bitterness and what Jesus bore for me. My steps lightened and I felt a sense of comfort: "For we do not have a high priest who is unable to sympathize with our weaknesses" (Hebrews 4:15).

My friend and I continued walking and talking and later stopped to pray. When we left the park, I was still hurting; I still felt some bitterness and anger; I knew that the journey ahead of me would not be easy. But I also knew that I would never be alone in my sorrow. Again the Lord brought to my mind that phrase "seventy times seven" and my need to obey and forgive.

I chose to forgive. My heart wasn't fully in it at first, but gradually the bitterness died out and love was replanted. Forgiveness is not just an emotion; it's a decision. Peter's words now have new meaning for me: "By his wounds you have been healed" (1 Peter 2:24).

Beyond Forgiveness

In your heart you know you have done right. You have obeyed God. You have forgiven. You have accepted the cost. You have, in a very small measure to be sure, experienced the kind of suffering Christ bore when He paid the price for your sins on the cross.

Be prepared. Your decision to forgive will be challenged. Some people may look at you as one who has played the part of a fool. Disruptive thoughts may tempt you to bring your decision up for further examination and severe questioning. Your emotional responses may not be positive right away. But be confident: In forgiving you have done the right thing.

In Part Two we will discuss ways you can defend your decision to forgive, deal with your conflicting emotions, and learn to love the offender through confrontation and reconciliation. As you move beyond forgiveness remember that the fruit of your righteous action will be peace, quietness, and confidence forever (Isaiah 32:17).

But before we move on to Part Two, there may be two other parties you need to consider. You may blame yourself or God for some of the pain and heartache you have suffered. You can forgive your parents, your spouse, your friends, and even nameless, faceless strangers for wrongs they inflicted on you. But if you don't learn to forgive yourself and don't cease blaming God, you will never be healed.

8

Let Yourself Off the Hook

*W*hen Beverly and Jim came to my office for pre-
marital counseling, both were visibly uneasy.
Beverly fidgeted with a piece of paper, and Jim stared
listlessly out the window. After we chatted a while, they
began to become more comfortable.

The questionnaires and tests they had completed
before this first session had already alerted me to a
problem that could devastate their prospective marriage.
It was clear that Beverly felt her life had been destroyed.
She saw her existence as simply a struggle to survive.

As we talked together, Beverly hesitantly answered
several open-ended questions I directed toward her.
Then I asked her to describe the home where she grew
up. There was no disguising the fact that Beverly was
crippled by the emotional pain of her youth. Taking a
deep breath, Beverly began to unfold the story of her
past.

Beverly became pregnant at the age of 16. Her pregnancy had been a prison sentence. Her parents acted as
the prosecuting attorneys, and she had no choice but to
become the lawyer for her own defense. She lost the case.
For nine long months she was sentenced to the solitary
confinement of her bedroom and the upstairs bath.

During her incarceration her parents hardly said a word to her. As far as they were concerned she was a hopeless disgrace. Beverly would never forget their rapid-fire remarks: "How could you do this to us? What will the neighbors think? Don't you care about our good name?"

The breech birth was excruciatingly painful for Beverly, but it was nothing compared to the anguish of having her baby taken away. The nine months of pregnancy seemed like an eternity, the birth was traumatic, and in the end Beverly's arms and heart were empty. The child she longed to love was gone.

Her parents' response, though expected, stabbed at her heart. They never even acknowledged the baby and wouldn't allow their "good name" to be printed on the door to her hospital room. The sign simply read, "Beverly."

She recounted the entire story without a tear. Beverly was beyond crying. She looked like a prisoner. Her hands gripped the arms of her chair like they were rigid cell bars. In her mind she was still imprisoned. She had given herself a life sentence; no time off for good behavior.

Beverly faced what may well be the most difficult kind of forgiveness: She had to forgive herself. The passing years had brought no relief from her unresolved guilt. Even her boyfriend's tender words hadn't set her free. Beverly had accepted all of the guilt her parents had piled upon her, and with the guilt came all of the pain.

Symptoms of Self-Condemnation

Beverly is an example of anger and unforgiveness turned inward. Call it self-condemnation. Self-condemnation produces the listless doldrums where your will to act is dormant. It is bitterness toward yourself that resides in a dimly lit chamber of your aching heart.

Are you imprisoned by feelings of self-condemnation? Have you been down on yourself in some area of your life for as long as you can remember? Whether your feelings are as severe as Beverly's or your bondage is more subtle, there are two warning signals that indicate you've failed to forgive yourself. The first is a constant striving for perfection in some facet of your life. You live your life trying to prove yourself to someone—but who? The second mark of self-condemnation is a chronic and crippling sense of personal guilt in which your conscience constantly accuses you.

Perfectionism. Are you locked up in the prison of performance? Are you constantly attempting to live up to some impossible level of achievement or conduct? Do you feel inescapable pressure to work for God's approval?

When you fail, do you feel compelled to try twice as hard? "I must make up for my failure," you tell yourself. No matter what you do it never seems good enough. Your compulsion to be perfect persists—and it's driving you crazy.

Tendencies like these, taken alone or in combination with other compulsive behaviors, condemn you to your own emotional prison. Your failure to forgive yourself places you in a torture chamber of your own design. By believing you can earn God's favor and forgiveness you have sentenced yourself to a life of dismal disappointment. The ticket to freedom is understanding and accepting how God views you and your sins.

Guilt. In my college days I worked as a psychiatric social worker. My responsibilities included evaluating disturbed and suicidal individuals for court-ordered, emergency hospitalization. I would interview both the patient and the family, then I would explain my findings before a judge.

In this role I saw firsthand how guilt destroys people. I remember evaluating a divorced woman with two children. After having an affair, the woman began to exhibit bizarre behavior. In her futile attempt to cleanse her life of her sins, she forced her children to take five showers a day. She also carried her couch outside and set it on fire because it reminded her of one of her sexual encounters. Guilt literally drove this woman insane.

Guilt is that gnawing sensation that says, "You were wrong." Like acid, it slowly eats at your spirit. The pain becomes a source of misdirected energy. Your family and friends describe you as driven and compulsive. Activity seems to soothe your guilt, at least temporarily. You keep yourself continually occupied so you don't have to be alone with your condemning thoughts. Your busyness is your feeble attempt to avoid facing head-on the real problem: the need to forgive yourself.

Why Can't You Forgive Yourself?

Every attempt to escape your guilt and self-condemnation by earning your forgiveness will fall short. So why do you keep trying? Because your self-justifying behavior rests on three crumbling pillars: a distorted view of yourself, a distorted view of your past sins, and a distorted view of your present relationship with God. To experience the joy and freedom of forgiveness you must stop trying to fulfill these distorted, self-imposed demands and accept God's perspective.

Your view of yourself is distorted. How do you view yourself? Against whom do you measure yourself to judge your success? There are two common mistakes we tend to make in evaluating ourselves.

First, we judge ourselves by the world's standards. The world says there is nothing worse than cellulite or underdeveloped pectorals. External appearance looms as one of our society's primary barometers of value.

But what does God say? "Man looks at the outward appearance, but the Lord looks at the heart" (1 Samuel 16:7). The implication is obvious: Your heart matters more than your external appearance. God doesn't care if you are a cover girl or Mr. America. The only thing that impresses Him is a pure heart.

So why do we have a virtual epidemic of Christian women fighting bulimia and anorexia? Because we have bought into the world's view of what is important. We're playing the comparison game by the world's rules, we are losing, and we can't forgive ourselves for our failure.

Second, we are deceived into a distorted self-view when we imagine ourselves to be independent and self-sufficient. This apparent self-sufficiency is really pride. When pride is at work, any failure comes as a shock to us. If we think we have it all together, any mistakes we make suddenly become larger than life. It's popularly termed "low self-esteem," but it's really pride.

Are you brooding over some past sin or personal failure? Why? Did you really expect sinless perfection? Did you really think you would never make a wrong move? If you have placed such unrealistic expectations on yourself, you have a distorted perspective.

Peter's life illustrates this perspective problem. He told Jesus he would die for Him. No personal cost was too great. Peter viewed himself as the perfect friend who would never let Jesus down. But only hours later Peter denied he even knew Jesus. Peter was weak, and Satan used Peter's pride to cause his downfall.

We are cut from the same human fabric as Peter. We too can easily be ripped apart in spiritual warfare. Have you lost a battle? Several, you say? So did Peter. So did Paul. So will you.

There may be one big difference between you and Peter: He faced his failure and accepted God's forgiveness. Though he failed miserably, God used him mightily.

He introduced 3000 people to the Savior on the day of Pentecost. He did not allow himself to be handcuffed by self-effacing pity. Peter nailed his sin of pride to the cross and got on with his life.

Your view of your sin is distorted. Perhaps you're thinking, "Well, God forgave Peter, but He won't forgive me, not after what I did." You can't forgive yourself because you don't believe God has forgiven you.

If you think that way, you're wrong. What is your "unforgivable sin"? Name it. Adultery? Do you remember what Jesus said to the woman caught in the very act of adultery (John 8:11)? Divorce? Do you remember that He ministered to a woman who had been divorced five times (John 4:1-26)? Murder? Do you remember what God told King David after he'd murdered Uriah to cover up his sin (2 Samuel 12:13)? Homosexuality? Do you remember what Paul said to the Christians in Corinth who had been homosexuals (1 Corinthians 6:9-11)? What about theft, alcoholism, slander, or embezzlement? Read 1 Corinthians 6:9-11 again.

If you are holding some sin against yourself, it's because you don't understand or you refuse to believe what the Bible says about forgiveness. Here's the truth.

First, *your sins are beyond reach.* When you seek God's forgiveness, He forgives and dismisses your sins. God's love for those who fear Him is greater than the distance from heaven to earth—immeasurable. His forgiveness separates our wrongdoings from us as far as the east is from the west—an incalculable span (Psalm 103:12).

Think of it this way: God didn't say He would dispatch our sins as far as the North Pole is from the South Pole. We can measure the span from pole to pole with incredible accuracy. But we cannot measure how far east is from west. God is saying, "Your sins are forgiven. They are beyond your reach. Even more than that, they are too remote for Me to touch them as well."

The question is obvious: Why try to grab hold of what God has purposely put out of reach? Why stand tiptoe at the top of a ladder, reaching for the sky? It's time to climb down and allow the cloudy memories of your old, dead sins to simply blow away.

Second, *your sins are out of sight*. Like us, King Hezekiah of Judah struggled with pride. His vanity showed when he pompously displayed Israel's golden treasures to an enemy nation. God's verdict: Hezekiah must die.

What sin had created, forgiveness could cure. Hezekiah repented before God and God forgave him. God the judge took guilty Hezekiah from the courtroom, led him into His chambers, and said, "I've placed your sins behind my back." God removed Hezekiah's sin from the record and canceled his death penalty (Isaiah 38:17).

God has placed your sins behind His back. He put Himself between you and your offense. Please believe it. Don't try to outmaneuver Him so you can see them again.

Third, *your sins have evaporated*. God sweeps away our offenses like a cloud that quickly passes from the sky. Just as the sun disperses the morning mist, God causes our sins to evaporate. He makes our sins disappear (Isaiah 44:22)!

The next time you find yourself flying at 30,000 feet, why not try grabbing a handful of cloud? I'm afraid you'll be disappointed. Why not do the same with your sins? Try to grab them, and you'll discover your hand is empty. They are gone like the wind, like a cloud, like the morning mist.

Fourth, *your sins are covered*. God doesn't remember our sins or count them against us. The payment of the blood of Jesus Christ covers all of our offenses (Isaiah 43:25; Jeremiah 31:34; Hebrews 8:12).

When you were a child, did you ever hide under the covers? You hid in order to be out of view, to not be found, to not be seen. In the case of your forgiven sins, the covers are permanent. You need not see them; you shouldn't see them. In fact, you can't see your sin any-more. Why? Because God's forgiveness covered it, and now it's gone. It's Satan, "the accuser of our brothers" (Revelation 12:10), who wants you to think God is still upset with you.

Fifth, *your sins have been dumped overboard*. Your sins have been thrown into the deepest recesses of the sea, far too deep to be dredged up or recovered (Micah 7:19).

Imagine yourself on a ship whose captain is Jesus Christ. You notice Him move toward the side of the ship with a bucket full of ugly, slimy, black rocks—your sins. He pours the whole lot into the sea. Far too heavy to float, they fall rapidly to the water and immediately dis-appear into the depths. They're gone forever.

Since God has dumped your sins into the sea, do you want to throw them a life preserver? Do you want to dive into the sea and try to rescue them rather than let them sink to the bottom forever? Of course not. Let them go and enjoy the cruise!

Sixth, *your sins have been sent away*. Your cheeks burn with shame as the men parade you to the temple square. They shove you along, shouting and cursing. A crowd quickly gathers. "Who is she? What did she do? What's going on?" they ask.

"A filthy adulteress!" the self-righteous rulers shout. "We caught her in the act! We're taking her to the temple to be stoned!" As the bystanders hear about what you did, they begin to slap you, call you names, spit on you.

You thought you already knew what humiliation was. You thought you knew how it felt to hate yourself. You didn't before, but now you do.

Finally you arrive at the temple. Jesus is there. The men who caught you say, "Teacher, this woman was caught in the act of adultery. In the Law Moses commanded us to stone such women. Now what do you say?" (John 8:5).

You know what He will say—the only thing He *can* say. The Law is unambiguous. But He doesn't say anything. He just writes in the sand. *Why isn't He giving them an answer? What in the world could He be writing?* A tiny hope awakens within you: *Maybe He's trying to think of some way to spare my life! Maybe He wants to give me another chance! Maybe He's writing the passage in the Law that can save me!*

Finally Jesus speaks: "If any one of you is without sin, let him be the first to throw a stone at her" (v. 7). One by one your accusers leave, fading away into the crowd. You think, *He's been writing down their sins!* Soon even the crowd is gone. You're alone with the man who saved your life.

He says, "Woman, where are they? Has no one condemned you?"

"No one, sir."

"Then neither do I condemn you. Go now and leave your life of sin" (vv. 10-11).

Imagine that the woman refuses to go. Instead, she still feels that she deserves to be condemned, not pardoned. She takes stones from the pile the men had gathered for her execution and throws them one by one into the air. It isn't easy, but she's able to get some of them to hit her as they come down.

That's preposterous! But some of us do the same thing. We continue to punish ourselves for sins God has long since sent away. Don't let that happen to you. Jesus has sent your sins away and freed you from the place of condemnation. Leave them behind. Don't try to go back. Don't pick up the stones.

God has ransacked the language of man utilizing numerous pictures to communicate, "Your sins are gone. There is no record of them, no memory bank, not even a 'dead file' in the farthest recesses of the archives of heaven."

This is the truth that caused the poets and hymn writers to pen words like, "How marvelous, how wonderful is my Savior's love for me" and "Amazing grace, how sweet the sound."

Your view of God is distorted. You may not be willing to forgive yourself because you don't feel that God is a gracious, forgiving God. Perhaps you've created your view of the heavenly Father from the image of a hostile earthly father. Maybe you see Him as downright hostile—the great Terminator, the omnipotent Ogre, the cosmic Ebenezer Scrooge who won't cut anyone a break.

Such an attitude is certainly understandable. God would be justified in simply throwing all of us into hell because we've all done wrong. We've actually *earned* everlasting punishment; it's *owed* to us (Romans 6:23).

But God has chosen to love us and provide a way of salvation for us. He sent His Son to collect our paycheck of death and award us His life instead. God is loving and merciful, wanting every human being to be saved from the penalty for sin (2 Peter 3:9).

There is only one way to learn this truth: Take it by faith. Believe what the Bible says about God:

> Do not fear, for I am with you; do not be dismayed, for I am your God. I will strengthen you and help you; I will uphold you with my righteous right hand (Isaiah 41:10).

> "I know the plans I have for you," declares the Lord, "plans to prosper you and not to harm you, plans to give you hope and a future" (Jeremiah 29:11).

> For God so loved the world that he gave his one and only Son, that whoever believes in

him shall not perish but have eternal life (John 3:16).

There is now no condemnation for those who are in Christ Jesus (Romans 8:1).

In all things God works for the good of those who love him, who have been called according to his purpose (Romans 8:28).

If God is for us, who can be against us? He who did not spare his own Son, but gave him up for us all—how will he not also, along with him, graciously give us all things? Who will bring any charge against those whom God has chosen? It is God who justifies. Who is he that condemns? Christ Jesus, who died—more than that, who was raised to life—is at the right hand of God and is also interceding for us. Who shall separate us from the love of Christ? (Romans 8:31-35).

No message is clearer in Scripture than the good news of God's love. Believe it. Accept His love and forgive yourself.

How to Forgive Yourself

Be certain of your salvation. To experience the freedom of self-forgiveness, first make certain you have personally trusted Christ as your Savior. The Bible explains that we have all done wrong (Romans 3:23) and have earned a place in hell—eternal death (Romans 6:23).

A perfect God cannot ignore your sins or pretend they didn't happen. Sin must be punished. But God loves you. He wants to rescue you from your sin and give you a place in heaven. So He sent His Son Jesus to take the penalty of eternal death you deserved (Romans 5:8). He died on a cross, paying the price for your wrongdoing, and three days later rose to life again—a total victory over sin, death, hell.

There's nothing left for you to do. Jesus has paid the entire price for your sin. His death for you is a free gift. All you have to do is receive it (John 1:12; Romans 10:13).

Place yourself on record with God. Tell Him that you are trusting solely in what Christ accomplished for you through His death on the cross for the forgiveness of your sins.

Forgive those who have wronged you. You will not overcome your self-hatred until you forgive those who have wronged you. If you feel bitter toward yourself, look for hidden bitterness toward someone else that you have redirected toward yourself. It's often easier for us to focus our anger, hatred, and bitterness on ourselves than to admit we have these feelings about others. When you have a grievance against someone you depend upon and love, it may seem safest to convince yourself this person didn't really wrong you or that the offense doesn't much matter. But in your heart you know it really does matter. You're angry and bitter, so you take it out on yourself.

That's what happened to Beverly, whose story I shared earlier in this chapter. Though at first she insisted she had no anger toward her parents for their hostility toward her, she eventually acknowledged that she was carrying resentment. By admitting her true feelings she took the first step toward forgiving herself.

It's time for you to admit your true feelings. Recognize the bitterness within you. If the person you're angry with actually did mistreat you, forgive him. If not, repent of the unfair perspective you've been treasuring in the hidden recesses of your heart. Ask God to help you from now on to admit and resolve bitter feelings rather than deny them and let them boomerang back to hurt you.

Confess and claim God's forgiveness. Confess any known sin to God. When you can't forgive yourself, you are saying, "I'm dirty." You may even be saying, "I'm so soiled and filthy I just know God is through with me." He isn't! If He were, you wouldn't be here; He'd have taken you to heaven (see 1 Corinthians 11:28-32).

You can become clean again. Here's how: "If *you* confess *your* sins, He is faithful and just and will forgive *you your* sins and purify *you* from all unrighteousness" (1 John 1:9 paraphrased, emphasis added).

You can forgive yourself when you are assured that God has forgiven you. He commands you to confess your wrongdoing to Him. Acknowledge your sin. Accept responsibility for those sins before God. Agree with God that these sins are vile and detestable in His sight and that they are primarily sins against Him. Affirm before God that your sins are the very sins for which Christ died. No matter who else is involved, be willing to say with King David, "Against you, you only, have I sinned and done what is evil in your sight" (Psalm 51:4).

"Isn't there something else I must do to be forgiven by God?" you ask. Nothing! God is faithful to you and righteous by His own standards when He forgives you and purifies you from your sin. God takes away the dirtiness and makes you clean. When you by faith come to God and confess your sins, He cleanses you. And if you are clean in God's sight, you are really clean.

Accept God's view of yourself. Who are you really? Is the real you the person you see in the mirror? Is it the person others see? Or is it the person God sees? Let God's view of you direct your thinking and your praying.

So how does God see you? The Bible makes this clear. From every page of the New Testament the Lord shouts out His exalted view of those He has saved through His Son. If you are a Christian, you can say—you must say— about yourself...

- I am a new creation (2 Corinthians 5:17).

- I am a child of God (John 1:12).

- I am God's handiwork (Ephesians 2:10).

- I am a citizen of heaven (Philippians 3:20).

- I am more than a conqueror (Romans 8:37).

- I am Christ's friend (John 15:15).

- I am the salt of the earth (Matthew 5:13).

- I am a joint heir with Christ, sharing His inheritance with Him (Romans 8:7).

- I am a temple of God; He lives inside me (1 Corinthians 3:16).

- I am united to the Lord (1 Corinthians 6:17).

- I am reconciled to God (2 Corinthians 5:18-19).

- I am one of God's holy ones (Ephesians 4:24).

- I am one of God's chosen ones (Colossians 3:12).

- I am a member of God's royal priesthood (1 Peter 2:9).

- I am free forever from condemnation (Romans 8:1).

- I am justified—God has declared me righteous (Romans 8:30).

- I am the dwelling-place of God's Spirit (1 Corinthians 3:16).

- I am blessed with every spiritual blessing (Ephesians 1:3).

- I am complete in Christ (Colossians 2:10).[1]

The myopia of a "poor self-image" fades away like the morning mist in the sunlight of these truths. God is making you like His perfect Son, Jesus Christ. Your destiny as a Christian is to bear His image. As you become like Christ, a little bit of heaven lives on earth.

Beverly finally learned this lesson. Her pregnancy stripped her of her dignity, leaving her an open target for the insulting arrows of her parents. She knew well that she could not regain her virginity, but she finally realized that through Christ's forgiveness she had regained her purity. Having experienced God's love and forgiveness, she forgave herself. So can you.

9

Do You Need to Forgive God?

*O*nce upon a time, your life was simple and uncom-
plicated. You managed well, balancing your hurts
with healings and your failures with fulfillments. But
that was before the unforgivable assault crashed into
your life. You may not have said it, but you came close to
saying it: "I don't know if I can ever forgive God for
allowing this to happen to me!"

The words "forgive God" sound so strange that they
defy explanation. But they express your feelings because
you know God could have arranged things to prevent
the offender from saying what he said or doing what he
did. But it happened—the heartless neglect, the cutting
words, the abusive deed. And you wonder, "If the
Almighty is really almighty, why did He let the roof fall
in on me?" You feel like there were two offenders: the
person who did the misdeed and God, who stood by and
let it happen.

It probably doesn't help you much for me to say,
"God can't sin, so He doesn't need your forgiveness."
You know enough about God already never to accuse
Him of sinning. What you are really saying comes from
your emotions, not your brain: "God, I don't think I can

handle the fallout from this disaster. I really wish You had prevented it!"

Now that's quite a statement in itself. Your estimation of God and your understanding of what He can do can't be faulted. He could have vetoed the entire fiasco before it ever materialized. You don't question His power, but you have some serious doubts about His love for you. You keep asking yourself, "How can God be a God of love if He allows others to hurt me so?" You say to God, "Why? Why me? I didn't do anything to deserve this. Why did You let it happen, God?"

It's difficult to describe the feelings of shock, bewilderment, emptiness, rejection, isolation, and even anger experienced when you are convinced that God has somehow been unfair with you or let you down.

Why God Lets Bad Things Happen to Good People

Yes, something very bad has happened to you at the hands of a hurtful person. You are in despair. You may be eaten up by bitterness or thoughts of revenge. And you continue to be mad at God for letting it happen.

The Bible tells us that bad things happen—even to good people. Cain murdered Abel (Genesis 4:1-8). Herod slew the innocent babies (Matthew 2:13-16). There are many other biblical examples of bad things happening to good people that parallel what has happened to you. Furthermore, God knows all about the the painful things that happen to you (Hebrews 4:13).

But the nagging questions remain: Why does He allow bad things to happen? Why did He allow this person to hurt you? Thankfully, the Bible gives us some answers.

God uses hurts to help us gain a correct perspective. There are two ways of looking at life: our way and God's way. The Bible helps us see the difference: "The Lord does not look at the things man looks at. Man looks at the outward appearance, but the Lord looks at the heart" (1 Samuel 16:7); "'For my thoughts are not your thoughts, neither are your ways, my ways,' declares the Lord. 'As the heavens are higher than the earth, so are my ways higher than your ways and my thoughts than your thoughts'" (Isaiah 55:8-9).

We don't see as God sees because our human nature clouds our view. We see life in human instead of divine terms. We look at life through the lens of time instead of eternity, law instead of grace, man-centeredness instead of God-centeredness. The best lens adjustment on our perspective is accomplished when we allow our trials and hurts to help us see people, circumstances, and problems from God's point of view through His Word.

Our faulty human perspective is often a result of being uninformed or misinformed about what's happening around us. In Psalm 73, the psalmist writes about how his perspective was changed. First, he looks at life through the human lens: "I envied the arrogant when I saw the prosperity of the wicked. They have no struggles; their bodies are healthy and strong. They are free from the burdens common to man; they are not plagued by common ills....Surely in vain I have kept my heart pure" (vv. 3,4,13).

Then his pain drives him to God and he begins to see things differently: "When I tried to understand all this, it was oppressive to me till I entered the sanctuary of God; then I understood their final destiny. Surely you place them on slippery ground; you cast them down to ruin. How suddenly they are destroyed" (vv. 16-19).

When someone hurts you, you may think, "I'm just as good as he is, even better. I don't deserve to be treated this way. I deserve better. I deserve more blessing." Are you viewing your circumstances through God's eyes or your own? Is the offender really better off than you are? The person who hurt you owes God for what he did.

Would you really rather be in his shoes? Adjust your perspective by filtering it through God's Word.

What we expect out of life also profoundly affects our perspective of our trials and hurts. We tend to expect immediate justice, solution, and gratification when we have been wronged. "God, I want the offender punished and my heart healed—now!" we insist. We have little tolerance for delay or disappointment. It is difficult for us to see God working through unpleasant circumstances when an instant miracle would be so much more convenient.

But we have no scriptural basis for expecting immediate, direct, divine intervention every time someone hurts us. Yes, our God is a miracle-working God. But He is also the God of providence—day-by-day provision and supervision of all people, circumstances, and things. God controls our calamity and our prosperity (Jeremiah 32:42). And He calls us to expect His provision even when we must persevere to receive it (Hebrews 10:36). As Jerry Bridges says in *Trusting God Even When Life Hurts*, "God's providence is His constant care for and His absolute rule over all His creation for His own glory and the good of His people."[1]

Through the experience of the painful offense, God is cultivating in you His perspective of you and the offender, and His provision for your healing.

God uses hurts to shape us. Remember the prophet Jeremiah? God gave him a message to proclaim to Israel about the abuses they were to suffer. Jeremiah was perplexed. Why would God let His people suffer so?

So what did God do? He told Jeremiah to get away from the crowd and go down to the potter's house (Jeremiah 18:1-6). There Jeremiah saw broken pieces of hardened clay, lumps of wet gray and tan mud—probably not an inviting scene. He saw the craftsman at his wheel. The wheel, so much like the fickleness of circumstance, kept turning. Jeremiah could identify his people with the broken, lumpy clay spinning on the wheel. There seemed to be no relief in sight for them, no getting off that wheel.

That may be the way you feel as you look at what's left of you after what you have suffered. Your life seems to be little more than a shapeless mass spinning in circles, going nowhere. It's undeniable: God let circumstances get out of hand. You were deeply hurt, and your outlook is bleak. You thought God was making something beautiful of your life. But the offense reduced you to an ugly, cold, hard lump.

You watch with Jeremiah as the potter kneads the clay into a workable lump and starts the process all over again. He cuts pieces off. The odd-shaped lumps fall to the mud floor. The treatment is rough. The clay still looks like your life, all right. It's all bent out of shape. Everything seems hopeless for that lump of clay and for you.

But the potter keeps working, and something wonderful begins to happen. The lump is taking shape. It looks different than it did before. It's even more beautiful. The potter has taken a broken, formless lump of clay and created a work of art.

Look at the hands that are shaping your life through the painful experience you have suffered. Look at the feet working the treadle. See the nailprints? The Potter knows about pain and abuse. He experienced rejection and hatred. Yet look what the Father created out of Christ's brokenness. And never doubt again that He can use your hurts to shape you into something even more beautiful and useful than you ever thought possible.

God uses hurts to teach us about Him. Also consider Job, who plummeted from health and prosperity to boils and poverty in almost no time and for apparently no human reason (Job 1:1–2:10). Human explanations for Job's suffering usually center on one of the following:

1. God is all-powerful, just, and fair, but Job was unrighteous. But the Bible states that Job *was* righteous, so that can't be the reason for his suffering.

2. Job was righteous, and God is all-powerful, but God is not just and fair. But this is unthinkable and contrary to the Bible. It's not the answer.

3. Job was righteous, and God is just and fair, but God is not all-powerful. But Scripture says otherwise. God is in control; He is all-powerful. Luke 1:37 says, "Nothing is impossible with God." When you inwardly blame God, questioning His control, you overlook His love, especially as it is expressed in John 3:15-17.

If you're tempted to blame God for what happened to you, you are underestimating the problem of evil in the world, which came by man's rebellion against God. Evil is a fact. We must face it. Evil, not God, influenced the offender to hurt you. God could have prevented it, but He didn't. He could prevent all evil from occurring simply by wiping out everybody. But He won't. The all-powerful, all-loving, just, and fair God allows evil to affect us to teach us about Him.

God answered Job's "why" questions simply by revealing more of Himself. God wanted to shift Job's attention from "why" to "who." Through Job's affliction God was communicating, "You won't understand why I allowed it, but you *can* understand that I'm in control. I'm working all the time." The whole story of the book of Job shows God working *behind* the scenes, God working *on* the scene, and God working *beyond* the scene.

Did Job receive satisfying answers to all of his "why" questions? Emphatically no. But he acknowledged and blessed the God who was in control of his circumstances.

He banked on God's sovereignty (Job 1:21; 2:10; 42:2). He refused to blame God (1:22; 2:10). He believed that a glorious resurrection was at the end of it all (19:25-26). And he bowed in worship and contrition to the One who was in control (42:1-6).[2]

In the midst of the pain of being offended, don't ask, "Why is God letting this happen to me?" Ask instead, "Who is in control?" God wants to show you His love and care, not by shielding you from pain but by loving you and preserving you through it. Acknowledge with Job that God is too kind to do anything cruel, too wise to make a mistake, too deep to explain Himself, and too near to be unaware of your need.[3]

Let God Off the Hook

When I was a young pastor, a very special elderly gentleman in the church was one of my heroes. George was a rugged sort who had an authentic twinkle in his eyes that would make every "Night Before Christmas" Santa drool with envy. In many ways he was still in his prime even at 74, and he had a crop of wavy white hair to top off the portrait of a vigorous, successful individual. He had made his living in the rough-and-tumble construction business.

George was an encourager. I remember thinking in my early days of pastoring, *This is the kind of man and the kind of deacon every church should have!* He was a tower of strength to me. He always seemed to have a tank full of joy. Life had been good to him, or so I naively thought.

It was at a men's fellowship meeting one night when George gave his testimony that I began to have some insight into my hero's rocky road in life. If I've ever met a modern-day Job, George was he! He had been married three times and had wept at the graveside of each of his three "life partners." He had not heard from one of his sons in more than 20 years, nor did he know his whereabouts. His daughters were alcoholics, and their lives brought shame to their loving, concerned father.

I was crying conspicuously by the time George concluded by saying, "Folks ask me how I can make it through all these trials. The best way I can express it to you is that I have found a place where I can get all the help I need. I know where that place is, so I go back there again and again. God has never failed me."

Here was a man with a heart broken many times over, but he had real joy! He knew where to turn with his grief—he knew *Who* to turn to. If George could shift his attention from "why" to "who," so can you.

How do we let God off the hook for the offenses we have suffered from others? We don't need to forgive Him because He did nothing wrong. But we may need to stop questioning Him and blaming Him and instead start affirming His justice, His love, and His sovereignty in our affairs. When times of trouble come your way, say:

1. I am here by God's appointment, in His keeping, under His training, for His time.

2. He brought me here. It is by His will that I am in this place. In this fact I will rest.

3. He will keep me here in His love and give me grace to behave as His child.

4. He will make the trial a blessing, teaching me the lessons He intends me to learn and working in me the grace He means me to bestow.

5. In His good time He will bring me out again. How and when, only He knows.

Forgiven and Forgiving

After reading through Part One, perhaps you're inclined to say, "I appreciate the work you have put into this book. I'm sure you know what the Bible says about forgiveness; I wouldn't argue with a couple of preachers about that! I know many people will find your book helpful. But not me.

"You see, what you say doesn't really apply to me. I simply *can't* forgive the person who wronged me. The hurt was so calculated, so brazen, so completely uncalled for. I don't expect people to be perfect. Lord knows, I'm no angel myself. But this time the skunk has gone too far.

"Having read the first half of your book, I see that in my heart of hearts I don't even *want* to forgive the person who has treated me so badly. But even if I wanted to, I don't see how I *can* let go of a hurt like this one."

If you feel this way, I understand. I've been on the receiving end of an "unforgivable sin" too, and I know what it feels like. But just the same, something is radically wrong with your spiritual life. God's Word is clear: Christians live a lifestyle of forgiveness. And there's a specific reason for that. Believers *forgive* all because we're *forgiven* all.

We realize that nothing anyone has ever done to us or will ever do to us can hurt us as deeply as our sins hurt Jesus Christ. He died for our sins when He had done nothing wrong, when He owed us nothing. We can never match the love Christ showed for us, but we can imitate it: "Forgive as the Lord forgave you" (Colossians 3:13).

If none of this rings a bell for you, if you simply can't work up any willingness or interest in forgiving the person who has wronged you, it's important to ask why. In fact, it's time to take the test Paul mentions in 2 Corinthians 13:5: "Examine yourselves to see whether you are in the faith; test yourselves."

Paul wrote those words to church members. They all thought they were Christians, but some of them thought wrong. They were counting on an emotional experience or church membership or their talents or their good character or being baptized or knowing Christian doctrine or following the Golden Rule to get them into heaven. They weren't counting on the one provision God made to bring them into His favor: the blood of Jesus Christ shed on the cross for the sins of men and women.

So if you really feel you can't forgive, *perhaps it's because you've never experienced God's forgiveness.* But I have good news for you. You can experience His forgiveness right now.

The Bible tells us that God is perfect and perfectly righteous. There's no way in a million years He could tolerate any sin at all. To ask Him to overlook a little bit of sin would be like asking a ship captain to overlook just a little bit of a hole in the hull of his ship. Some things are unacceptable in any quantity. To God, sin in any quantity is unacceptable.

And since you—like everyone else—have sinned, and God can't just overlook your sin, He can't accept you. He must condemn you to spiritual death, which means never-ending torment and separation from Him (see Romans 3:23; 2 Thessalonians 1:8-9; Revelation 20:15). Nothing you can do can change this verdict because nothing you do can take away your sin. You can't undo your sin any more than you can unscramble an egg. People try to pretend they can be good enough to please God, but this gambit only insults Him: "All our righteous acts are like filthy rags" (Isaiah 64:6).

But what we cannot do, God has done. He has provided a way to take away our wrongdoing and forgive us. He sent His Son, Jesus Christ, to die for our sins on the cross and raised Him from the dead to give us His life here on earth. Christ, the eternal Son of God, became a human being like you and me. But unlike you and me, He lived a sinless life. He did not deserve death, but He *voluntarily* died in the place of sinners. As Romans 5:8 says, "God demonstrates his own love for us in this: While we were still sinners, Christ died for us." Isaiah 53:5-6 expresses the same idea: "But he was pierced for our transgressions, he was crushed for our iniquities; the punishment that brought us peace was upon him, and by his wounds we are healed. We all, like sheep, have gone astray, each of us has turned to his own way; and the Lord has laid on him the iniquity of us all."

If you will admit that God is right in finding your sins intolerable, you can accept Jesus Christ as your Savior. God will accept Christ's death as full payment for everything you ever have done wrong and everything you ever will do wrong. Your unforgivable sins will be forgiven, and you will become God's friend—a friend to the Creator and Judge of the universe. You won't suffer everlasting torment and separation from God; you'll enjoy an eternal heaven with God.

If you're not sure you've ever really been forgiven, I urge you to put your trust in Jesus Christ right now. Rely on His sacrifice on the cross—and nothing else—for salvation, and you will receive God's full forgiveness. As Acts 16:31 says, "Believe in the Lord Jesus, and you will be saved." Similarly, John 3:16 states, "For God so loved the world that he gave his one and only Son, that whoever believes in him shall not perish but have eternal life."

Have you trusted in Christ as your personal sin-bearer? If you have, you are now forgiven. You've become a friend of God. You'll go to heaven when you die. In fact, you've become God's own child, as John 1:12 tells us: "To all who received him, to those who believed in his name, he gave the right to become the children of God."

Now you can forgive the unforgivable in others because you have been forgiven the unforgivable.

If choosing to forgive were all that was necessary to respond to the incident of neglect or abuse in your life, we could end the book right here. But it isn't. Even after you decide to forgive, which you must, how will you follow through with your decision? How will you put your emotions back together? What will you do about confronting the offender for what he did? Should you seek to reconcile your relationship with the offender? In Part Two we will deal with these important questions as we learn to love again.

_____PART 2_____

Learning to
Love Again

10

Maintaining a Forgiving Heart

*K*im and Kathryn are sisters. Apart from the alliter-
ation of their names, they bear no resemblance to
each other and have little in common. While growing up
they also grew apart primarily because their mother
played favorites. Kim was the apple of mom's eye and
Kathryn was treated almost as an afterthought.

Mom's obvious disdain sent Kathryn into a tailspin
early in her teen years. It wasn't until she turned 30 and
had her own children that she was able to forgive her
mother and her sister. When Kathryn told me her story, I
felt that she had really released her mom and sister from
the vast array of offenses that had accumulated over the
years. From what I could tell, her forgiveness was heartfelt.

Yet Kathryn sought my counsel because she was still
struggling with the mental and emotional anguish of
having been the black sheep of the family. When holi-
days approached, Kathryn started to relive some of the
painful memories of the past. Anxiety welled up within
her as she anticipated what might happen or be said at
the family gatherings.

At the close of one session she said to me, "I feel like
I am in bondage and I don't know what to do." These

are the words of a sincere, committed Christian who is dealing with the difficult realities in the wake of an offense, even one that has been forgiven.

Have you ever expressed to God your willingness to forgive someone's offensive behavior and then found yourself struggling with thoughts and emotions that begged you to renege on your decision to forgive? If your answer is yes, you are not alone. Furthermore, your feelings are not wrong. Face it: Forgiveness *has* happened, but the battle isn't yet over. A serious challenge remains—to follow through with your decision to forgive, and maintain the spirit of forgiveness in order to love again.

Four major concerns must be addressed in order to move beyond forgiveness so that you can love again. First, you must defend your decision to forgive the person who has offended you when you face the temptation to entertain a grudge. Second, you must determine how to resolve the residual emotional pain from the offensive incident. Third, you must prayerfully consider if God wants you to lovingly confront the person who injured you. And finally, you must answer the question "Can my relationship with the offender be reconciled and restored?"

Beginning with this chapter and continuing through Part two, we will address these four concerns: Maintaining forgiveness, resolving emotional pain, confronting the offender, and entertaining reconciliation. Dealing with these areas will help you love again.

Guard Your Heart

Does God expect you to forgive a person for some horrendous affront and then moments later embrace that person as if nothing had happened? No! God is a realist, and He knows that in some situations this would only invite another assault. His counsel is clear: After you for-give, guard your heart.

After forgiving someone, we should heed the admo-nition of Proverbs 4:23: "Above all else, guard your heart, for it is the wellspring of life." The Spirit of God makes this a priority "above all else." If we do anything, we are to guard our hearts by building a wall of protection against an attack on the very core of our being.

This same advice was given to the wayward priests of Israel who had abandoned their wives for the women of other nations. God Himself testified against them because they had broken faith with their wives. While they were being tempted to dissolve their marriage covenants, God gave them the solution: "So guard your-self in your spirit, and do not break faith with the wife of your youth" (Malachi 2:15). How were they to guard their spirits? By agreeing to honor their commitment and by distancing themselves from the source of their temp-tation. Like the priests of Israel, we are to take whatever steps are necessary to protect ourselves from temptation. The priests were to avoid being enticed by other women, and we are to circumvent situations where we would be prone to renege on our decision to forgive.

If you are being harassed by sinful emotions, imme-diately look for ways to guard your heart. If an encounter with the offender entices you to develop an unforgiving spirit, stay away from that person. Give yourself space and time to anchor your feelings in the Word of God.

A pastor's teenage son was publicly rebuked and later "piously" prayed for by the youth pastor. The teen admitted his anger and prayed with his dad to forgive the youth pastor for what he had done. He even agreed that he would need to talk with the youth pastor about what had happened.

The following Sunday, this young man told his dad he didn't want to go to church. He was afraid he might get angry at the youth pastor and say the wrong thing. It was an emotionally sensitive time for him, and he needed some time and distance to gain a better perspective. He was guarding his heart in order to maintain forgiveness.

Like this young man, it may well be that you need the opportunity to stabilize your emotions before having another encounter with the person who hurt you. Admit your vulnerability, and then consider what you need to do to guard your heart. If a face-to-face meeting at this time would threaten your act of forgiveness and throw you into a tailspin, look for ways to maintain your distance.

There are several guidelines that may assist you as you guard your heart.

Keep your goal in mind. Guarding your heart is neither a pious form of retaliation nor an attempt to run from your offender. You simply want and need some time to stabilize emotionally so you are better able to safeguard the forgiveness you have already extended.

View your caution as a short-term need, not a long-term response. If you try to guard your heart by saying to yourself, "I'll never talk to her again no matter what happens," you are wrong. Or if you pull your church membership five minutes after you have been maligned by a church leader, you are wrong. Don't do it in the name of guarding your heart.

Remember: All you want is a little bit of time to get your emotions under the control of the Holy Spirit so you can respond to the offender in love.

Don't guard yourself as a form of subtle retaliation. When you feel God would have you maintain some distance from the other person, don't do so as a counterattack. If at all possible, don't even speak to the other person during this time. But if you find yourself in a situation where you must either run or face the person, consider the encounter as a divine appointment and extend a cordial greeting.

Don't be naive. Genuine forgiveness is not gullible. Although unconditional love "always protects, always trusts, always hopes, always perseveres" (1 Corinthians 13:7), we also are fully aware that sinful patterns don't simply disappear when we forgive an offender. There are people who are trapped in sin (Galatians 6:1), repeating episodes of infidelity, drunkenness, or outbursts of anger.

Forgiving another does not guarantee that mistreatment will end. Forgiveness frees us to respond in a positive and biblical way, but we shouldn't expect the other person's harmful behavior to simply disappear because we did what was right.

So, if someone continues to direct sinful actions toward you, be on guard emotionally. At the same time, recognize that something must be done to help that person break the sinful pattern. God may eventually want you to confront the one who offended you. But before you do, you will more than likely engage in the spiritual struggle that typically follows in the footsteps of forgiveness.

Expect Inner Turmoil

Our old sin nature generates ideas that trigger negative emotions (Romans 7:18; Ephesians 2:3). Sin within us will challenge every positive response we make toward the Word of God. It is a relentless war. On one side we feel a strong pull toward hatred, discord, fits of rage, dissensions, and factions (Galatians 5:19-21). On the other side we feel the tug toward peace, patience, kindness, and gentleness (Galatians 5:22-23).

When we forgive, we live according to our Christlike nature and choose peace. At the same time, the sin nature within us counterattacks with a strong drive toward resentment and indignation.

Have you ever experienced this inner turmoil? The apostle Paul knew the same struggle. Apply his words to your desire to honor your decision to forgive: "I have the desire to do what is good, but I cannot carry it out. For what I do is not the good I want to do; no, the evil I do not want to do—this I keep on doing" (Romans 7:18-19).

This inner strife comes from a desire that cannot be reconciled. Your sin nature desires to get even, while the Holy Spirit wants you to walk in love. The sin nature and your new nature are in conflict, so you sometimes do what you don't want to do (Galatians 5:17).

We might paraphrase and apply Paul's words this way: "For I have the desire to love again, but I cannot carry it out. Disruptive memories and negative thoughts and feelings overwhelm me."

Expect your sin nature to harass you. Anticipate an assault on your mind designed to compel you to relive past offenses that you have already forgiven. But with the help of the Holy Spirit, you can continue to walk in Christlike love and forgiveness.

Stand Your Ground Against Satan

Our sin nature makes it difficult enough to follow through on forgiveness. To make matters even worse, Satan, the enemy of our souls, is the master of accusation. In fact, he is even called "the accuser" (Revelation 12:10). If anyone can challenge our decisions to forgive, Satan can and will. Paul wrote, "Our struggle is not against flesh and blood, but against the rulers, against the powers, against the world forces of this darkness, against the spiritual forces of wickedness in the heavenly places" (Ephesians 6:12 NASB). Satan has his forces. They are a horde of fallen angels or demons. We are in a lifelong campaign against this Satan-led militia.

Have you ever considered what Satan uses to attack us? His assault on us is likened to "flaming arrows" that can and must be extinguished (Ephesians 6:16). These missiles are often ungodly thoughts directed at our minds and designed to disrupt us emotionally and spiritually.

The late Merrill F. Unger, one-time professor at Dallas Theological Seminary, had a very balanced view of spiritual warfare. In the late 1970s he wrote *What Demons Can Do to Saints*. From his vast experience and knowledge, Dr. Unger noted that evil spirits attempt to influence our minds, our wills, and our emotions. He went on to say that demonic activity of this nature is common among Christians.[1]

Evil spirits cannot read our thoughts, but they *can* place ideas into our minds which are contrary to what God's Word says. Our struggle with the forces of darkness revolves around Satan's ability to mislead and deceive us, and he does so with mind games.

Satan knows that if he can direct our minds he can also control our lives. Consider Ananias and Sapphira, who openly professed to be Christians and who were part of the early church (Acts 5:1-11). After selling a piece of property, this couple gave part of the proceeds to the apostles, apparently saying that they were donating the total purchase price. They lied. Why? Was the sin of greed at work? No doubt. But there was more. Peter said, "Ananias, how is it that Satan has so filled your heart that you have lied to the Holy Spirit...?" (v. 3).

How did Satan fill their hearts? How did he entice them? Satan used deceptive thoughts to set on fire negative emotions and gain control over Ananias and Sapphira. Imagine how he whispered his malignant thoughts into their ears: "Ananias, you worked hard to get that land. Don't give all the money away. Just give enough to look good in the eyes of the apostles. Sapphira, that money is your security, your nest egg. What if Ananias dies? Who will take care of you? Why not give just part of the money? How will they know the difference?"

Consider the parallel to your life. The Holy Spirit brought you to the point of forgiving the one who offended you. Now Satan wants to challenge that decision. Mind games. Strong appeals to your sin nature. That's Satan's strategy. And when it comes to forgiving someone else, he uses the same tactic in an attempt to undo your decision to forgive.

Can you hear his voice? You may be in a situation where you can't forget the pain of your wife's infidelity. Satan whispers in your ear, "Does God really expect you to let her off the hook after what she has done?" When you encounter the brother who defamed your character, Satan utters a taunt, "Did you see him smiling? See, God isn't going to bring justice to bear upon him for what he did. If you don't retaliate, nothing will ever be done about it."

Can you hear the accuser doing what he does best? He wants you to join him once again in pointing the finger at the person you have already forgiven.

You may be faced with a husband who is battling alcoholism. Satan's counsel: "It's going to happen again and again. Stop being a doormat and get out of this mess. You don't have to live this way." After a verbal battle with your mate, Satan will prod, "God doesn't really care about you or your marriage. If He did, He wouldn't allow these conflicts to happen."

How are you going to respond when Satan attempts to refill your heart with bitterness? Will you heed his endless accusations and innuendos? Will you renounce your decision to forgive? Will you allow your negative emotions to get the better of you? You should not and need not. You can stand your ground and defend your decision against the accuser. How? By bringing your thoughts under the control of the Holy Spirit.

Capture Your Thoughts

What you think generates how you feel. Ideas have consequences. Your thoughts ultimately determine your emotions. If your emotions are to be securely anchored after you've forgiven someone, proper thought patterns are absolutely essential.

One of the clearest statements of this principle is found in 2 Corinthians 10:5: "We demolish arguments and every pretense that sets itself up against the knowledge of God, and we take captive every device of human reasoning and obey Christ."[2] We are to trust Christ and follow Him alone. The key to following through on your commitment to forgive is to capture every thought and subject it to the person of Christ and to the truth of the Word of God. Paul commands us to capture wrong thoughts and destroy them.

There is no thought that is beyond God's reach. Paul said, "He catches the wise in their craftiness....The Lord knows that the thoughts of the wise are futile" (1 Corinthians 3:19-20). As you learn to love again, you will be engaged in a spiritual battle. You must get your thoughts right by making sure they are aligned with God's Word.

If you are alert and on guard, you will be able to evaluate the thoughts that come into your mind. If you search the Word of God you will be able to compare all thoughts with the truth. In order to live a godly life, you must capture the thoughts that come from the world, the flesh (your human nature), and the devil. You must demolish any satanically inspired thought process. Submit these evil thoughts to capital punishment. Destroy them with a vengeance. Then you must replace the evil arguments and pretenses (fakery) with two mandatory Christian military disciplines: meditation upon God's Word and implementation of God's truth in your life.

Jesus Christ gives us the best illustration of this important truth. Whenever He was challenged to do something that was not right, He came against it with the Word of God. He did this repeatedly in the desert wastelands where He was tempted by Satan (Matthew 4:1-11). Satan appealed to some of the basic desires of Christ's humanity. Jesus responded to each false thought with the truth of the Word of God. You can do the same when Satan appeals to your old nature to go back on your decision to forgive.

Imagine that your ex-wife has turned your children against you. You have sought forgiveness for the wrongs you did, and you have forgiven your wife for her offenses against you. But now, years later, the hostility over these incidents resurfaces.

It's Christmas Day, and you are driving over to pick up your children for the afternoon. When you arrive, the usual tension is in the air. Your ex-wife gives you that nasty look and says, "Wasn't it enough that you ruined our lives? Now you're going to ruin another day."

A thought pops into your mind in response to her comment. You have the urge to fire back an equally cutting barb. Is that thought from God? Obviously not. It finds its source either in Satan or in the sin nature that is still at work in you (Romans 7:20). But you have decided, having already forgiven your wife, that you are going to capture thoughts like these and put them to death. You will not allow these thoughts to control your emotions. Instead you will bring them into obedience to your commitment to Jesus Christ (2 Corinthians 9:13). When you recognize the attack and you turn to Him, the fleshly thoughts are demolished in His presence.

By taking your thoughts captive in this way, you erect a barrier between the hurts you have suffered in the past and the temptation to take revenge in the present. You protect the forgiveness you previously granted, and you refuse to return insult for insult (Romans 12:17). As you continue to take your thoughts captive to the Savior, your mind embarks on a wonderful process of change.

Renew Your Mind

If you have a limited understanding of God's truth, you will have great difficulty recognizing a counterfeit thought. The command from God's Word is precise: "Do not conform any longer to the pattern of this world, but be transformed by the renewing of your *mind*. Then you will be able to test and approve what God's will is—his good, pleasing and perfect will" (Romans 12:2).

Every thought that comes into your mind must be tested to see if it is responding obediently to the will of God. In order for this to happen, your mind must be programmed by the Word of God rather than by the world's thoughts. If you are going to solidify your decision to forgive someone, you must allow your mind to be refreshed and renewed by the Scriptures. You must read the truth every day in order to recognize error. And as your mind is renewed, your emotions will become the product of right thinking. Your feelings will be in tune with God's Word.

Here's how a renewed mind captures thoughts with the weapon of truth:

- "I have been abandoned, and no one cares about me." Wrong! God said, "Never will I leave you; never will I forsake you" (Hebrews 13:5).

- "I have been abused, and no one understands." Error! Jesus understands. He was "tempted in every way, just as we are—yet was without sin" (Hebrews 4:15).

- "I have been slandered, my reputation is destroyed." No way! God's Word declares, "If God is for us, who can be against us?" (Romans 8:31).

- "I have been unfairly judged and made the object of ridicule." Captured! "He will bring to light what is hidden in darkness and will expose the motives of men's hearts. At that time each will receive his praise from God" (1 Corinthians 4:5).

As you continue to capture your thoughts by using God's Word, you will find that your emotional hurts will start to heal. As you allow your mind to be in the process of renewal, your emotions will be calmed, and "the peace of God, which transcends all understanding, will guard your *heart* and your *mind* in Christ Jesus" (Philippians 4:7).

As you seek to maintain a forgiving heart, what should you do about the inner wounds you suffered at the hands of the person who wronged you? Will these wounds ever go away? Is emotional healing a fantasy or a reality? In the next chapter, we'll find out.

11

Healing Emotionally

*T*he memories are etched on my mind and my heart. To this day I don't understand what happened, but I do know that it deeply wounded me and my family. I doubt that I will ever forget the flood of tears and the sensation that my emotional agony would somehow consume me.

On more than one occasion I asked the Lord "Why? Why me? Why this?" The reason: He wanted this book to be hammered out on the anvil of experience. These truths had to be tested in our lives before God would allow us to share them with you.

The most difficult lesson I have had to learn is how to deal with the emotional anguish that lingers when you have been devastated by another person's actions. Feelings such as anger and despair seem to have a mind of their own. When you least expect it, they steal your joy and peace. Somehow they can invade even your best days and most restful nights.

Do you know what I mean? Have you ever cried yourself to sleep at night agonizing over what happened between you and another person? Have you ever hurt so much that you didn't know how to pray? Do you remember sensing that you were so helpless that you

131

needed the Holy Spirit to pray for you and intercede on your behalf? Have you ever wondered if the anxiety would ever go away?

It's Gone Forever

It's important to remember that your emotions are not the barometer of forgiveness. There are people who find virtually complete emotional relief when they release someone else through forgiveness. But Scripture does not guarantee instantaneous relief. If it happens, great; but don't count on it. For most of us, emotional healing will take time and a special touch from God.

Israel's Day of Atonement (National Day of Forgiveness) beautifully illustrates the contrast between instant forgiveness and gradual emotional healing (Leviticus 16; Hebrews 9:1-14). Imagine yourself near the temple mount in Jerusalem. The priest is leading two goats to the temple. One will die in a kosher procedure: The sacrificial knife slits its jugular vein. This goat is sacrificed for the sins of the people. Its blood is taken by the priest to the Most Holy Place where it is sprinkled on the altar in the presence of God. All sins are forgiven before sundown that very day. The sprinkling of the animal's blood on the altar closes the case on all offenses.

But what about the second goat? What part does it play in this drama of forgiveness?

The priest turns from the slain goat to the goat that is still very much alive. He places his bloody hands on the head of this goat, representing the transfer of sins from the people to the goat. This goat, sometimes called the scapegoat, is then led into the wild and barren mountains southwest of Jerusalem. At intervals along the path to the wilderness, sentries observe the goat's journey.

Eventually, word of the goat's release in the wilderness is signaled back to Jerusalem from watchman to watchman. The scapegoat will never be seen again. This report is greeted with shouts of joy and thanksgiving. "The scapegoat is finally lost in the wilderness," the people cheer. "It's gone forever. Our sins are gone!"

Think of the two goats as the phases of forgiveness and healing. The first is a ransom goat. The instant death of this goat symbolizes immediate forgiveness. The second goat is the release goat. The banishment of this second goat to the uninhabited wilderness requires time and effort. This second goat pictures the assurance of eventual—rarely immediate—emotional well-being after you have forgiven someone.

Focus your binoculars on this second goat as it departs and finally disappears from view. Look for the signal flags of the sentries waving back the message, "The goat is lost in the wilderness. It's gone forever." There *will* come a time when your emotions *will* subside. You will remember what happened, but the pain will be gone.

The Road to Emotional Healing

Are you ready to send that second goat into the wilderness? Then consider several essentials on the road to complete emotional recovery.

Expose your heart to God. A prerequisite to emotional healing is honestly telling God how you feel. Do you find this hard to do? It may be your lack of faith or a hidden resentment toward God because you are disappointed that He allowed you to be slandered, insulted, or abused. Could it be that you are angry at God and refuse to divulge your inner thoughts? Why not be sincere with Him about your disillusionment? More than once I have said to the Lord, "I cannot for the life of me understand why You have allowed *this* to happen. It makes no sense at all." Do you know what I have discovered? When I am honest in my despair, the Lord meets me right where

I am. Before long I can cry out with the psalmist, "Trust in him at all times, O people; pour out your hearts to him, for God is our refuge" (Psalm 62:8).

From personal experience I have also found that emotional pain can either drive a wedge between me and God or become a vise that presses me closer to Him. It all depends on how I respond. Sometimes I allow myself to wallow in my own frustration, keeping God at a distance. At other times I have been totally transparent and have cried out to God in my distress. His love is always there when I am on my face before Him weeping and feeling helpless and completely dependent. Whenever I expose my heart to Him, I experience His compassion and care.

If you are carrying some heavy hurts, don't read another word before telling the Lord how you feel. Be honest. Be transparent. Be real. Remember: He is the Physician of your soul.

Endure your pain to the glory of God. "But it hurts so much. I can't stop crying. I am physically and emotionally spent. It all seems like such a waste." Yes, it will be a waste if your agony remains your own. You must give your pain to God as a sacrifice.

There is a way to redeem what you're going through. God wants you to trust Him in the hard times. He wants you to rely on His love and goodness when life doesn't make sense. When you are devastated and yet still turn to Him, He is pleased.

You may feel like you are a slave to all your pain and hurt. Thoughts of the person who offended you may bring you into weariness and depression. But it's precisely when you feel like somebody's slave that the Bible speaks to your feelings and says to you:

For this finds favor with God: If a man bears up under the pain of unjust suffering because he is conscious of God (God's presence and awareness of your heartache). But how is it to your credit if you suffer for doing wrong and endure it? But if you suffer for doing good and endure it, this is commendable before God. To this (endurance through suffering) you have been called. Because Christ suffered for you, bearing your sins in His own body on the tree (cross), leaving you an example, that you should follow in His steps (1 Peter 2:19-21, author's paraphrase).

Approach your distress as:

- a circumstance designed to draw you closer to God.

- a special occasion to vividly remember Christ's sufferings on the cross for you.

- an opportunity for you to entrust yourself to a loving God who judges justly, as Christ entrusted Himself to the Father when He died for your sins.

You can redeem your suffering to the glory of God, and that will also open the door for you to experience in full measure His incredible love.

Cast your cares on Christ. Emotional healing occurs when you place your inner pain at the foot of the cross. It was the apostle Peter, who so often struggled with his own emotions, who wrote, "Cast all your anxiety on Him because he cares for you" (1 Peter 5:7). When your emotional pain begins to burden you and anxiety wells up within you, at that very moment throw them on Jesus. Why? Because He genuinely cares, and He *will* carry your burdens for you.

First Peter 5:7 expresses the New Testament equivalent of what King David wrote: "Cast your cares on the Lord and he will sustain you; he will never let the righteous fall" (Psalm 55:22). This verse pictures a man walking in the desert carrying a heavy pack upon his shoulders. An Arabian tradesman comes alongside him and invites the man to throw his load on the camel. Similarly, the Lord is both willing and able to bear even your heaviest burdens, even when you feel as though you are lost in the desert without so much as a canteen of water. God will sustain you and keep you from becoming weak and faltering along the way.

At this point you may be saying to yourself, "But how can God care for me when I've done so many things wrong?" Have you stopped to think about what Peter did wrong? In Jesus' hour of great need, Peter betrayed Him. When Jesus asked for prayer, Peter was one of those who fell asleep. Even after Jesus' resurrection, Peter was the one who was unable to say how much he really loved Jesus. Yet years later Peter was able to write that Jesus cares.

Jesus cares for you no matter what you have done or what others have done to you. He desires to carry your anxiety and your pain. When you cast your cares on Jesus, you are fixing your eyes on Him, the author and perfecter of our faith. You are looking to the One who endured pain for you. He encourages you to stay on course and never give up (Hebrews 12:2-3).

But how do you cast your cares upon Him? Simply turn to Jesus in your moment of intense need rather than try to carry the burden alone.

Marie knew she could not shoulder the emotional weight of her husband's infidelity. She had forgiven Joe for several episodes of adultery over a period of some ten years. Steps were taken to strengthen their marriage and to help Joe deal with his sin.

But one night, several weeks after his last affair, Joe made obvious amorous overtures toward Marie. Marie's mind was pelted with thoughts and images of the other women. Her mind raced. *Will he be thinking about them instead of me?* Her heart tried to keep pace with her mind, and anxiety seized control. She was able to leave the room before Joe saw her tears.

Alone in the bathroom, she cried, "Lord, I have forgiven him. Help me love him again." Her cry for help was answered. She regained her composure and spent a delightful evening with her husband. God's peace was evident.

You can cast your painful emotional burden and anxiety on Jesus by a simple, heartfelt prayer. As you pray, believe that He receives your burden and carries it for you. Walk away in peace.

Find a burden sharer. When we cast our cares and burdens on the Lord, He may well bring into our lives someone who can directly share in our suffering. Although my wife is my best friend, God has also graciously given me a couple of men that I count as "blood brothers." In each case, the relationship was forged during a time of intense emotional pain.

My friendship with Bill began when the ministry of The Art of Family Living faced the possibility of closing. The board asked Bill to help respond to what seemed to be an insurmountable financial need. Bill brought his faith and financial insights to our ministry, and before long he had encouraged me and stabilized the financial foundation of our outreach.

Another friendship I deeply value is with Irv, a man I got to know when his 37-year-old brother Bob was dying of cancer. The Lord allowed me to be part of this difficult but triumphant time in the lives of Irv and his family. I provided emotional support at that time, and he has returned the blessing many times since.

My friendship with Ron Brame grew as his wife Kathy courageously battled brain cancer. Facing her own mortality, Kathy came to know the Lord and amazed everyone as she walked in the peace and power of God. Her life so radiated the person of Jesus Christ that her husband Ron agreed to go with her to church. One Sunday morning, with Kathy at his side, Ron bowed his head and asked Jesus Christ to be his Savior.

Kathy lived longer than the doctors thought she would and, undaunted by the cancer, was able to bring two beautiful children into the world. Over the years, and especially during Kathy's final days here, I was able to share in Ron and Kathy's personal pain.

Despite the burdens Ron has had to carry, he now lifts me up when the weight of the ministry becomes almost unbearable. In fact, it was Ron who reminded me of Ecclesiastes 4:9-10: "Two are better than one, because they have a good return for their work: If one falls down, his friend can help him up. But pity the man who falls and has no one to help him up!"

With Bill, Irv, and Ron, I have learned the importance of friendship and the need to "carry each other's burdens...and fulfill the law of Christ" (Galatians 6:2).

When you are suffering, don't go it alone. If you need help, admit it. God wants to provide help and His method may well be a friend who will stand with you and for you.

Keep a pure heart toward the offender. People with problems tend to lash out at others. Their response to their own distress is often to inflict harm on people around them. Think about the offenders in the Word of God. Cain got angry when God did not accept his sacrifice, so he killed Abel in a fit of rage and jealousy (Genesis 4:2-8). Joseph's brothers resented their father's affection for Joseph, so they sold him into slavery (Genesis 37:23-27). King Saul was a man trapped by pride and harassed by an evil spirit. In his agony of soul he repeatedly tried to kill David (1 Samuel 18–19) and even turned against his own son, Jonathan (1 Samuel 20:30-31).

You can help resolve your own misery by trying to see the spiritual poverty in the life of the person who offended you. You are well on the road to healing when you honestly start to feel compassion and sympathy toward that individual.

Express your kindness for the person who hurt you by doing what is best for him. In Proverbs we read, "If your enemy is hungry, give him food to eat; if he is thirsty, give him water to drink...and the Lord will reward you" (25:21-22).

Place value on the one who hurt you. Valuing others is the essence of love. Because we love the offender, we refuse to fight him. Instead, we react in a loving, caring way, no matter how we feel. This is not an exercise in hypocrisy. It is simply the dynamics of what happens when true love confronts hate.

Pray for the offender. King David wrote, "Wicked and deceitful men have opened their mouths against me; they have spoken against me with lying tongues. With words of hatred they surround me; they attack me without cause. In return for my friendship they accuse me, but I am a man of prayer" (Psalm 109:2-4). Notice how David responded to being attacked: He prayed for his assailants.

Praying for our offenders is not just a good idea; it is commanded by Jesus Christ: "Love your enemies and pray for those who persecute you" (Matthew 5:44). As you pray, expect God to work in the relationship.

One of the richest blessings of our radio ministry is receiving countless letters from listeners who tell us wonderful stories of the grace of God at work in their lives. One day a member of our staff came to me and said, "John, you have to read this letter." It was a letter from a woman named Linda.

Linda described how her unbelieving husband, Jim, left her for another woman. She remained single and faithfully prayed for Jim for 15 years while he was living with the other woman.

Then something incredible happened. Jim became a Christian after his long-term, live-in partner died. Jim and Linda renewed their marriage vows and enjoyed 17 years of oneness in Christ. Linda wrote to us after Jim's death from cancer. In her letter she reflected on what had happened: "The years we had together were worth the wait. Now I know my precious husband is in heaven. This is what I prayed for all along—that Jim would find Christ. I wouldn't trade anything for these last 17 years, especially the privilege of helping Jim during his terminal illness. I look forward to the day when I will be with him again and forever."

Have you prayed for the person who injured you? Why not begin today? You may be amazed to find out what God will do in your life as well as his.

Entrust judgment to God. When you are praying for the one who harmed you, you may want to ask God to bring the relational problem to speedy resolution by judging the offender. Hear the words of the psalmist: "Awake, and rise to my defense! Contend for me, my God and Lord. Vindicate me in your righteousness, O Lord my God; do not let them gloat over me" (Psalm 35:23-24).

The apostle Paul was a great forgiver. He forgave those who abandoned him (2 Timothy 4:16), and he also forgave and was later reconciled to John Mark. Paul also had to deal with the lingering pain of being mistreated and, in working through his anxieties, he consciously entrusted the outcome of his being offended to God.

In 2 Timothy 4:14, Paul is very candid about his feelings: "Alexander the metalworker did me a great deal of harm. The Lord will repay him for what he has done."

Notice the apostle's honesty as well as his willingness to allow God to be the final judge.

While I was in graduate school, I worked part-time at a Christian organization. Unfortunately, my immediate supervisor proved to be unethical and, as a result, made life miserable for me. Rather than fight, I simply left and found another job. His actions jeopardized me and my family's welfare. I left wondering if this man would ever be found out.

Many years later I got my answer. The man's life was in shambles. When I heard the news I can honestly say I felt sorry for him. No doubt God was dealing with him, and it was an utter tragedy.

When your emotions encourage you to pick up an offense you have already forgiven, entrust the offender and what he did to the Lord. Don't be haunted by your memories. Instead, trust God to be the righteous judge.

Look beyond the immediate problem. There is a confidence that God wants you to have in the midst of your emotional holocaust: "He who began a good work in you will carry it on to completion until the day of Christ Jesus" (Philippians 1:6). God uses tough times to complete His perfect work in us. That's the perspective you need as you face each day.

But there is also a future perspective that is essential to your emotional healing. Some of us will face a lifetime of suffering. Our misery seems to be endless. It is precisely at this point that our vision must extend beyond this life to the next, as we remind ourselves that "our present sufferings are not worth comparing with the glory that will be revealed in us" (Romans 8:18).

I can still see Joanne's face as she looked up from her hospital bed. She knew that she had just a few days to live. She looked over at her husband Bob and said, "Honey, I want to go home." He knew the home for which Joanne longed. Soon she realized her heart's desire and complete freedom from the physical torment of her cancer.

As you resolve your own personal, inner agony, keep your eyes on "home" and expect God to translate your pain into another person's gain. A hurt that has been healed becomes hope for another person in need.

Anticipate the good that will come. Are we really willing to believe that Romans 8:28 is true? Do *all* things work together for good? If you are having some doubts meet Dr. Helen Roseveare.

Helen studied at Cambridge University in England and was converted to Christ through a campus ministry. She was single and just 29 years old when she dedicated her life to serving the Savior in Africa. Helen served as a medical missionary in the Congo (now Zaire) in the 1960s. While overseeing a 100-bed hospital and leprosarium, she treated as many as 250 patients a day.

In 1964, a revolution broke out in the Congo. A marauding rebel army swept through the country on a rampage. One night Helen's home was surrounded by the rebel forces. One of the leaders entered Helen's home and forced her into her bedroom and demanded that she undress. As she did, he pushed her onto her bed and brutally raped her. She survived what seemed like an eternity of mental and physical abuse, only to be thrown into prison where again she was raped.

Could any good possibly come from the horror experienced by Dr. Roseveare?

When the rebellion ceased, Dr. Roseveare courageously returned to Zaire and completed a total of 20 years service in that troubled and needy nation. Following her work there, she was commissioned by the Worldwide Evangelization Crusade and acted as a spokesperson at missionary conferences around the world. Over the years Dr. Roseveare has challenged thousands of students to serve the Lord as missionaries.

While addressing one such conference, Dr. Roseveare sensed a strong urging from the Holy Spirit to share the account of being repeatedly raped. She obeyed the Spirit of God, and described how she had been violated and shared how the grace of God was the source of her healing.

After the meeting was dismissed, two young university women sought her out. One was weeping hysterically. Through her tears this broken girl recounted how she had been sexually attacked five weeks earlier and had buried her pain and shame by refusing to tell anyone.

Dr. Roseveare placed her arms around this young woman and held her close to her heart. Dr. Roseveare knew then that her dreadful experiences many years before were her "credentials" to comfort this young lady.

That night, Dr. Roseveare understood better than ever the words of the apostle Paul: "Praise be to the God and Father of our Lord Jesus Christ, the Father of compassion and the God of all comfort, who comforts us in all our troubles, so that we can comfort those in any trouble with the comfort we ourselves have received from God" (2 Corinthians 1:3-4).

God wants to use you and even your most traumatic experiences to help others. His specialty is taking something grim and making it great. Are you willing to trust Him?

As your inner pain begins to subside, and it will, you need to address another important issue. Having forgiven the offender and beginning to deal with your emotional pain, you need to determine if you should confront the person who wronged you.

12

When Does Love Confront?

*T*o many, Louise is a perfect wife, a great mom, and a wonderful grandmother. Her husband reached the pinnacle of success at an early age, and people who know Louise recognize that she deserves more than half the credit for his accomplishments. She is poised and elegant, as comfortable in high society as she is at a church picnic.

But Louise has a problem, a problem that only her family and a few friends know about. Louise is an alcoholic who looks for life's meaning at the bottom of a bottle. Her grandchildren never get an answer to their question, "What's wrong with Grandma?"

We know from the previous chapters that God's Word is clear: Louise's husband and children need to forgive her for the pain and embarrassment she has caused them over the years.

Do you have a Louise in your family? Maybe you're hurt because your husband is married to his job and neglects you and the children. Could it be that a member of your family is putting you through terrible torment because of substance abuse? Your child may have deeply hurt you by marrying someone whose lifestyle is diametrically opposed to yours. Or perhaps your child didn't finish college as you'd hoped, and things just aren't the same between you. Do you have a deep wound caused by a family member's gambling? Are you crushed because of an unfaithful spouse? Does the one you love have a problem with an explosive temper and cutting language, and you and other people are constantly in pain from his thoughtless, caustic remarks? Has someone at church or work misjudged your motives and told slanderous lies about you?

The raw reality of such misguided deeds brings us to another critical question: Should you confront the person who hurt you?

Many Christians have the false concept that forgiveness means allowing offensive behavior to continue undisturbed. I know of a husband who continually abused his wife in myriad ways, but in the name of submission and forgiveness she allowed his behavior to go on and said nothing, contrary to the advice of her pastor. Finally she reached the end of her rope and exploded, "I can't take this anymore. I quit! Sign the papers. Our marriage is over!" There is a strong possibility that the right kind of confrontation could have avoided the resulting divorce.

There are immature and rebellious Christians who sometimes claim "the Lord's leading" as justification for mistreatment of others. That, of course, is both foolish and sinful. In contrast, some Christian leaders today are inclined to disregard or even deny the Holy Spirit's ministry of guiding us in our Christian life. But the Bible teaches that God desires to lead us in our walk, and we need to rely on His leading to discern whether or not it is appropriate to confront a wrongdoer (see Psalm 23:2-3; Proverbs 3:5-6; Romans 8:13-14; Galatians 5:18).

Remember: Confrontation is not a scriptural requirement for forgiveness. Trust God through the Holy Spirit to reveal His perfect will to you about this matter, and then willingly follow His leading. As you seek His guidance, be mindful of the reasons love confronts and also keep in mind the reasons love does *not* confront.

Reasons Love Confronts

Confront to help the offender change. Do you know someone who often tells half-truths about other people to make himself look good and to make them look bad? He obviously has a distorted picture of himself or a problem with pride. When confronted with some of these half-truths (and even outright lies), he mumbles feeble excuses.

Ideally, when confronting an individual about his sin, your prayer is that he will change his mind about his behavior (that's what repentance is) and make a real effort to abandon his sin. You speak the truth in love, praying that the Lord will open the offender's eyes, and that he will really desire to become a totally honest person. Let him know, in love, that you want to help him change and be what God wants him to be.

If, deep in your heart, your real intention is to set the person straight, I caution you to hesitate and think twice before moving ahead. Your motives must be sincere or the confrontation will simply be a veiled form of vengeance.

Confront for the benefit of those being offended or when innocent lives are in danger. Obviously, if the person who offended you endangered your life and continues to do so, you must confront him immediately. If he persists, due to a mental, spiritual, or substance abuse problem, seek the proper authorities to deal with him.

You also have a responsibility to speak up when other people are in danger. Tragically, innocent children are abused in our society, and this horrendous reality continues at least in part because some people don't speak up. We know that physical and sexual abuse cannot be tolerated, and neither can ongoing verbal assaults. You must take a stand if you encounter situations where innocent or helpless people are being endangered. God will show you if you or someone else must do the confronting, but don't let it continue.

In Proverbs 6:16-19 we have a list of sins that are detestable in God's sight. Among them you find "hands that shed innocent blood" (v. 17). God wants to use you to help the helpless. His heart is revealed in the words of the psalmist: "Defend the cause of the weak and fatherless; maintain the rights of the poor and oppressed. Rescue the weak and the needy; deliver them from the hand of the wicked" (Psalm 82:3-4).

A dear friend took this admonition to heart and wrote a letter that demonstrates both the freedom of forgiveness as well as the need to confront a child abuser. Her letter reveals hope and healing while also demonstrating the courage it takes to confront.

Dear Mark,

I once trusted you. I loved taking tractor rides through the woods, climbing the big tree in your backyard, and picking fresh corn from the neighbor's garden for dinner. I wanted you to be related to me, taking the place of my natural grandfather who died when I was too young to remember him.

I don't remember exactly when I began to fear you. I tried to explain to Mom that I didn't like the way you kissed me. But since I was so young and didn't know how to explain myself adequately, she brushed off my complaints with comments like, "Oh, he's just very affectionate."

I began to dread visits to your house, but I was confused because no one else seemed to sense that something was amiss. I began doubting myself, thinking maybe the problem was with me. I never wanted to be alone with you, but everyone else thought you were just being kind when you invited me to the basement, the room above the garage, or for a walk in the woods.

I remember purposely tucking in my shirts and wearing heavy clothes so it would be more difficult for you to put your hands on me. I remember you chasing me around the ping pong table. I knew what you wanted to do, and I tried to postpone it as long as possible. I remember you making me sit on your lap or putting me on the shimmy machine while you put your hands up my shirt. I also remember you pinning me down on the floor with my legs spread apart, and you lying on top of me, feeling me out and forcing your tongue into my mouth.

What could possibly have made you do things like that to a 10-year-old girl, especially one who adored you and treated you like a grandfather?

You had no right to do that to me, and I hope to God that there weren't many other innocent children who suffered at your hands while you deceived their parents like you did mine.

I'm over being mad at you, and now I just feel sorry for you. I know that none of this was my fault. For my own peace of mind, I wanted to let you know that I've come to grips with what you did to me and how you took advantage of my innocence and trust. Lucky for me that my family came through in the end and put a stop to your abusive behavior. With their support I've grown up quite sane and sound.

Lucky for you that God doesn't hold a grudge, and that He has the ability to forgive even a child molester like you. If God can forgive, then I can too.

Patricia

Confront self-destructive behavior. A woman came to me concerned about her husband. She said, "I think I need to do something." I asked her what was going on. She said her husband had been arrested for driving while intoxicated. I asked if this was an isolated problem.

It wasn't. She revealed that her husband had several alcohol-related accidents and was also suffering from cirrhosis of the liver. And she was asking me if she should do something!

If someone close to you has a serious addiction that threatens his health and safety or the health and safety of other people, do something. Confront him about it. Don't wait until it's too late and all you have left is a lifetime of regrets.

One night following the midweek service, a friend of mine came up to me and said something about my message. I didn't hear a word Eric said because the alcohol on his breath was so strong I almost passed out. I realized Eric had a problem that could destroy him and his family.

Over the next few weeks I looked for an "open door" to say something. But while I delayed, Eric kept drinking, putting himself, his job, and his family in jeopardy. Fortunately, another friend saw the need for immediate action and intervened. Eric picked up the pieces of his life. To this day I regret that I waited.

Is there someone you need to confront, but you hesitate to do so because you know it will be difficult? Take my word for it: The price of waiting may be far greater than stepping out in faith and gently confronting your wayward friend or relative.

Confront in relationships where you are responsible. In certain relationships God has given you a measure of authority over people. For example, you have God-ordained authority for the care and protection of your children up to a certain age. When your child or someone else under your charge has a critical problem, don't avoid your obligation to confront.

A child's rebellion is an example of an offensive behavior a parent cannot ignore. In ancient Israel rebellion was dealt with in the strictest of terms. If a parent was unable to counter the child's rebellion, the child was to be stoned to death. I imagine that one or two stonings a year did wonders for improving the behavior of Israelite children!

Our method of confrontation today is not the same, but the importance of dealing with sinful behavior in those for whom you are responsible is still critical. It's often easier to overlook a serious sin in the life of a loved one. But don't be what is called today an "enabler." Confront, if you are responsible for that person.

In the book of Leviticus we have a stern warning: "Rebuke your neighbor frankly so you will not share in his guilt" (Leviticus 19:17). We are responsible for the actions of others, and this passage makes it clear that if we fail to rebuke, we share in the guilt associated with the person's misdeeds. To sit idly by means we are personally implicated.

Because of this truth, I am very careful when I send someone to a counselor. Candidly, I have been burned in the past by counselors who took advantage of the people I had referred to them. Several times I've had to contact a certain counselor because of his questionable behavior or unscriptural advice. As far as the Scriptures are concerned, we have no choice about confrontation. Speak now or share in the guilt.

Confront for the possibility of reconciling the relationship. Confrontation is hope for change and restoration when love and friendship have been destroyed (or at least put on hold). You have forgiven the person, but the previous closeness is not there. The breach has caused a void that is hindering your complete healing. A loving confrontation may be necessary if reconciliation is to take place. There are situations where, if the person doesn't change, reconciliation will be virtually impossible. We will deal with reconciliation more fully in chapter 14.

Reasons Love Should Not Confront

Real love is willing to confront. But real love is also willing to remain silent and avoid an untimely or unwise confrontation, no matter how tempting it may be to speak up and try to straighten things out. God's Word describes a number of situations in which we should avoid confronting the wrongdoer. In some of them the Lord's prescription for solving the conflict may come as a surprise to you!

Don't confront if you aren't certain you are the person to do it. In many cases confrontation may be called for, but you are not the person who should do the confronting. The most obvious case is where the problem or dispute is simply none of your business. As Proverbs 26:17 says, "Like one who seizes a dog by the ears is a passer-by who meddles in a quarrel not his own." I have never tried to pick up a dog by the ears, but I doubt this verse intends to commend the practice.

Often it seems noble and virtuous to intervene in someone else's quarrel. But unless you have specific authority to do so, God's Word says your involvement is folly. Don't fall into that trap.

Don't confront if you are uncertain of the facts or haven't really been wronged. Proverbs 18:13 states, "He who answers before listening—that is his folly and his shame." Don't rebuke a person for apparent wrongdoing until you have ascertained the facts as fully as possible. Too many friendships have been destroyed over alleged offenses that never occurred—either there was a misunderstanding between individuals or a third party injected disruptive gossip.

I recall reading about a man who arrived home late one night to find a supposed burglar standing in the darkness of his apartment. Only after beating the intruder mercilessly did the enraged man discover that he had entered the wrong apartment. Think about that the next time you hear a report of wrongdoing. Be sure you have the true facts before you confront.

Don't confront if it's more reasonable to overlook the offense. No matter how annoying or personally offensive you may find them to be, certain offenses are simply not worth making a fuss about. Sometimes the most loving response is no response at all. Just overlook or ignore the offense!

Proverbs 10:12 puts it this way: "Hatred stirs up dissension, but love covers over all wrongs." The apostle Peter echoed Solomon's wisdom: "Above all, love each other deeply, because love covers over a multitude of sins" (1 Peter 4:8).

You have a perfect right just to forgive and then drop many of the offenses against you without confronting the offender. Frequently it's the best course: "Starting a quarrel is like breaching a dam; so drop the matter before a dispute breaks out" (Proverbs 17:14). Let's face it: Rebuking a friend may be hazardous to the health of your relationship. Many attempted confrontations have quickly degenerated into quarrels. If at all possible, overlook the sins of others, especially sins of the tongue (see Ecclesiastes 7:21-22).

Even when your rights have been violated, don't forget your responsibility to set aside your own rights for the benefit of others. The Bible stresses this repeatedly but never more pointedly than in Philippians 2:3-8, where we are told to imitate Christ's example of giving up His rights for the sake of sinners.

Setting aside your rights for the benefit of a nonbeliever is an action for which the Lord will reward you.

In His Sermon on the Mount, Jesus explained how this behavior exhibits God's love and mercy to the world:

> Do not resist an evil person. If someone strikes you on the right cheek, turn to him the other also. And if someone wants to sue you and take your tunic, let him have your cloak as well. If someone forces you to go one mile, go with him two miles....Love your enemies and pray for those who persecute you, that you may be sons of your Father in heaven. He causes his sun to rise on the evil and the good, and sends rain on the righteous and the unrighteous (Matthew 5:39-41,44-45).

In the past, one of our neighbors purposely tried to antagonize me and my family. He complained when our boys played in the driveway when they were little because they made noise. He objected to us parking our boat on his side of our property because rats might nest under it. He ran an extension of his downspout onto our property so the rainwater would drain off his roof into our yard. His harassment really annoyed us, but we said nothing in hopes that sometime we could put a word in for Christ.

When his girls became old enough, his wife asked if they could attend Pioneer Girls and VBS at our church even though they were of another faith. This may never have occurred if we had allowed him to "get our goat" as he tried to do. It was worth the minor problems to be able to share the Savior with that family. This proved to us that it really was best just to drop the many issues and put aside our rights.

Don't confront if the consequences of the confrontation outweigh the offense. "An offended brother is more unyielding than a fortified city, and disputes are like the barred gates of a citadel" (Proverbs 18:19). There are two ways of learning this truth: You can read it in Scripture or you can discover it from personal experience. I recommend that you accept God's Word for it.

Particularly in the home, maintaining fellowship and harmony is more important than almost any other issue. Before confronting your husband or wife, mother or father, sister or brother over an issue that you predict will cause major sparks to fly, ask yourself, "Is raising this matter really important enough to risk splitting the family apart?" Sometimes it is (see Matthew 10:34-39), but most times it's not.

Does God's Word really put so much emphasis on maintaining peace at home? I'd like to answer that question by citing another principle which is wiser to learn from Scripture than from personal experience: "Better a dry crust with peace and quiet than a house full of feasting, with strife" (Proverbs 17:1). When you're tempted to endanger the harmony of your household by raising a touchy issue, try living on nothing but dry bread crusts for a few days.

Naturally there *are* many times when a confrontation at home is a must, regardless of the cost of peace for the family. The Holy Spirit will guide you when that is the case.

I find no substitute for the Spirit's guidance in discerning whether confrontation or forbearance will most effectively communicate God's character to other people. But if we err, let us err on the side of forbearance. Paul expresses it this way: "Bless those who persecute you; bless and do not curse." Peter wrote, "Do not repay evil with evil or insult with insult, but with blessing, because to this you were called so that you may inherit a blessing" (1 Peter 3:9; see also 1 Peter 2:19-23). Spend much time in the Word and in prayer concerning whether or not you should confront the one who has hurt you.

You now understand that there are situations in which love goes beyond forgiveness to confront the offender concerning his hurtful behavior. Once you recognize a situation in which someone you know must be confronted, you need to know how to confront in love.

13

How Love Confronts

When the Holy Spirit directs you to confront some-one, several issues must be carefully considered. First of all, you must be sensitive to timing and ask your-self, "When do I confront?" Before you move ahead, you must also determine the best way to approach the person. Take into consideration that you are seeking to honor the Lord in this effort. Finally, you must decide in advance what you are going to say to make this a profit-able endeavor.

Galatians 6:1 provides us with some key answers to issues like these: "Brothers, if someone is caught in a sin, you who are spiritual should restore him gently. But watch yourself, or you also may be tempted." These words apply particularly to the responsibility of con-fronting other Christians, but this passage is invaluable in considering your response to any offense that demands a rebuke.

When Are You Ready to Confront?

Is your heart right? Galatians 6:1 points out that "you who are spiritual" are qualified to confront and restore a brother caught in a sin. You must be under the control of the Holy Spirit before you are ready to confront and help restore another brother. This doesn't mean you have to wear a muzzle until you become a spiritual giant. But it *does* mean that you aren't ready for this solemn task until you are abiding in Christ, until you know His Word, and until you want to live for Him. If you are not spiritually ready, your attempt at confrontation will not be Spirit-led. In your own strength, you may not be gentle enough and your approach may not be appropriate.

Examine yourself first. If your marriage is a mess and you are faltering spiritually, you have no right to confront anyone. If you do so while in such spiritual jeopardy, the tendency will be to judge harshly and inappropriately. In fact, you will simply inflict your own frustrations on the person you are confronting, which will come off as a personal affront rather than a sincere challenge to change.

Are you ready to ask for forgiveness? In almost all conflict situations there is some wrong on both sides. One of the best ways to prepare for a confrontation is to admit your own guilt to the Lord and then to the offender when you confront him. When you ask for forgiveness for your wrong (even if it's only your unkind words when you were hurt), the offender's heart may be softened, and you will be better able to help him deal with his own failure.

One night over dinner Gary, a gifted physician, shared with me a traumatic experience from his childhood. This very competent and successful man demonstrated a tender spirit as he openly recalled the pain of his teenage years. Gary's mother and stepfather had carted him off to live with his father. Decades later, the sting of being rejected by his mother could still be heard in Gary's voice.

As we talked, I sensed that Gary needed to lovingly approach his mother in order to seek resolution and, hopefully, reconciliation. When I suggested to him that he write her a letter and apologize for anything he might have done wrong, even as a young man, his mouth dropped open. Even before I said a word, the Holy Spirit had placed the same burden on Gary's heart.

When you ask for forgiveness for your failure, you will help the other person deal with his failure. If you are unwilling to address your own sin, you have no right to attempt to help someone else address his sin (Matthew 7:3-4).

Do you really care about the offender? You cannot speak the truth in love unless you truly care. Such concern can only come from spending much time in prayer, asking God to give you a tender heart toward your offender. Ask God for the correct timing and an open door for you to be able to speak lovingly to the person who has hurt you.

Because of the depth of your care for this person, the thought of confrontation will probably be very distasteful to you. You may be so emotionally involved with him that the prospect of confronting him will make your stomach churn. But because you care, you are willing to put yourself through an ordeal that perhaps you would much rather avoid. If the thought of confronting another person sounds enjoyable, make sure to check your motives. If true love exists, you will find confrontation to be a very difficult task.

Are you sensitive to the offender's pain? In a previous chapter, we discussed the often-hidden pain of the offender. Be very sensitive to this as you confront and respond. The hurt in the life of the offender may blind his eyes, keeping him from objectivity when confronted and causing him to lash out at you even more. Don't be discouraged if he unleashes a fresh set of sharp words that spring from his own deep-seated agony.

What Type of Confrontation Is Appropriate?

When you think of confronting someone, a face-to-face meeting between two people usually comes to mind first. Obviously, a personal encounter is the most intimate form of communication. Personal contact allows you to ascertain how well your message is being understood, whether or not it is being accepted or rejected, and what is being communicated through his body language. It also allows for important interaction between the two of you.

Distance may make an in-person confrontation impossible, and there are other instances when it is just not practical. There are times when the meeting promises to be too emotionally or physically difficult or perhaps even dangerous. I've heard of countless women who personally confronted their husbands or boyfriends only to be savagely beaten up. In cases like these, a telephone call or a letter is a wiser choice.

When King Saul was intent on murdering David, there were no telephones. But David maintained a similar margin of safety when he confronted Saul by staying out of spear range and shouting his message (1 Samuel 26:13-24). Meeting in a public place may provide some protection from dangerous physical and emotional excesses.

A person may have such deep feelings of hurt or intense desires for healing in the relationship that he is unable to control his emotions and, thus, is unable to communicate effectively. To be in the physical presence of the person you're confronting is just not part of the solution at that time.

A personal letter is a very effective way to handle a confrontation and may prevent you from a hasty, unloving, or uncalled for confrontation. Writing also brings a sense of completion for having said your piece: "There it is; I've said what I had to say; I did what God wanted me to do."

Only after doing a lot of thinking and making notes should you begin your letter. Once you have written the letter, be sure it communicates your love and concern for the person while also asking forgiveness for the wrongs you have committed.

Never send a letter in haste. Ponder over it. Sleep on it. Be sure it says what you want it to say, reflecting your kind and gentle spirit, yet speaking the truth. Writing forces you to examine your thoughts. When you see your words on paper, they sometimes jump back at you. You may realize, "Maybe I'm to blame. Maybe I'm at fault at least as much as he is." You may even decide that a confrontation is not necessary. Writing will help you place a healthy distance between your words and your emotions. An unpleasant flare-up may be avoided.

A letter also allows the person confronting and the person being confronted reasonable control over the timing of the confrontation. Once you have written your letter, you can wait until the appropriate time to send it or present it, saying something like, "I would like you to read this letter when you get a chance, and pray about what I have said." The recipient then has the option to wait and read the rebuke when he's emotionally—and, ideally, prayerfully—ready to consider what it says. The Holy Spirit can bring him back to that letter again and again until its caring message does its work in his heart.

Many times over the years I have written a letter to someone who deeply hurt me only to find that, after rereading it, I felt better about the whole situation. Putting my thoughts on paper helped me clear the air. I still knew that I had been wronged and had offered forgiveness in my heart before God. But often the still, small voice of the heavenly Father told me not to send the letter. "Leave the matter and the judgment in My hands," He has said to me.

In 2 Corinthians, the apostle Paul provides us with a striking example of confrontation by letter. Paul had been planning to visit the believers in Corinth when he learned of a serious disorder among them that required a rebuke. But because of previous painful encounters with the Corinthian believers, Paul was unwilling to put them through the emotional turmoil a personal confrontation would bring: "It was in order to spare you that I did not return to Corinth....So I made up my mind that I would not make another painful visit to you" (1:23; 2:1).

Instead, Paul dispatched a strongly worded letter that resolved the problem. Paul's message in written form was very painful for the Corinthians: "Even if I caused you sorrow by my letter, I do not regret it... because...your sorrow led you to repentance. For you became sorrowful as God intended and so were not harmed in any way by us" (2 Corinthians 7:8-9).

Writing a letter is an approach to confrontation commended by both common sense and biblical example. But even if you decide that a face-to-face confrontation is the best approach in your situation, try to incorporate some of the advantages of a letter. Carefully think through and jot down what you want to say, what response you are likely to receive, and how you will respond—and pray, pray, pray!

How Do You Speak the Truth in Love?

When you confront someone face-to-face or by letter, there are several crucial choices you should make that will spell the difference between reconciliation and resentment. By planning to confront in a loving, God-honoring manner, you can avoid or minimize damage to your relationship with the wrongdoer and make it easier for him to repent and abandon his sin.

Begin with a sincere statement of love. Like a broken arm or leg, a fractured relationship causes excruciating pain. The person you are about to confront may be hurting inside. So open your letter or meeting by sincerely communicating your love for him. Let me emphasize the word *sincere*. Don't be a pious-sounding fraud and say you love the person when deep down all you really want to do is put him in his place. Tell him you care about him, you understand how he feels, and you want to honor his feelings. Then allow your loving commitment to the offender to set the tone for your entire encounter.

We've mentioned before that it is also necessary that you ask for forgiveness for your part in the problem. However unjustified the other person's wrong behavior was, you must let him know that you are sorry if you did or said something offensive to instigate or encourage that behavior. This doesn't make his actions right, but it does help you avoid a prosecutor's stance.

Focus on the positive. When you confront those who have hurt you, accentuate the positive elements of your relationship. Emphasize the good things you still have going for you. Share some of the positive memories you have in common. Reflect on the good deeds of the other person. He's not all bad, regardless of how much he has hurt you. For every word of criticism you plan to say, first speak ten words of encouragement. If you can't, don't move ahead. Your negative approach will do more harm than good.

Communicate clearly and honestly. As you speak the truth in love by mentioning the offense, be specific, straightforward, and frank, but gentle. Describe the situation as you really see it. Don't expect the other person to be a mind reader. Say something like, "I love you. But you're hurting our children and driving them away when you constantly put them down for not following instructions. You are so quick to criticize them and seldom really nurture and love them. You never spend quality time with any of us. You are always so tired and short to everyone. You're going to lose your children's love and do irreparable damage if you don't help me cultivate a happy family life for them."

Don't dwell on the pain you have suffered. This puts the focus on you instead of on the offender's need to repent and change.

Consider what the offender has to say. Whenever you confront someone in person, be ready to listen. The book of James warns us, "My dear brothers, take note of this: Everyone should be quick to listen, slow to speak and slow to become angry" (1:19). Furthermore, as you listen be ready to change your perspective on the offense. Even if you did all you could to get the facts straight before your meeting, you may have missed a key piece of information that will give you an entirely new perspective on the conflict.

You may not be able to agree with the other person's viewpoint, but if you are not ready to listen sympathetically, you're not ready to confront.

Challenge and encourage the wrongdoer to grow and change. Lovingly point out the positive behaviors and attitudes that should replace the sin. The New Testament repeatedly demonstrates this principle. Ephesians 4:28-32 teaches: *don't* steal, but *do* work with your hands so you can share with the needy; *don't* speak unwholesomely, but *do* speak what is helpful and beneficial; *don't* be bitter and angry, but *do* be kind and compassionate;

don't brawl, slander, and bear malice, but *do* forgive one another.

In the marriage relationship, you may be able to encourage growth more by asking questions than by demanding change. For example, you may say something like, "Honey, that remark you made about my weight in front of our friends last night really cut me. I want to be careful to build you up in front of other people. Will you help me do this? Will you commit yourself to building me up in front of others too?"

Commit yourself to change. When you follow God's revealed will in your interaction with people, much conflict becomes avoidable. Agree to do what God says to help bring harmony in your relationship (Proverbs 16:7). If you and the person you confront hope to enjoy the full fruits of reconciliation, both of you must be committed to obeying biblical commands. In the course of discussing an offense, you will likely hear about things in your own life that need changing. Rather than reacting to these accusations with insecurity and defensiveness, accept them at face value. Take them to God in prayer. Seek His counsel in the Bible. Commit yourself to godly change.

Close with a pledge to patience. There's no need to demand or expect an immediate response to the concerns you express during a confrontation. The Holy Spirit has been working in your heart; now allow Him time to bring conviction to the other person. Only He knows how far the other person has come in the journey toward repentance and reconciliation. If and when your offender repents, it's in God's hands, not yours. You desire a sincere change of heart; allow God to handle the timing.

Don't be surprised if the offender's first response to your loving rebuke is hostile. My wife has confronted me on a number of occasions. I needed it, but I can't say

I really liked it. At times I received her counsel very poorly. But time makes a great difference. I hear the rebuke, the Spirit nurtures it over time, and I change. Allow God to do the same in the heart of the person you confront.

The Outcome of Confrontation

I'd like to be able to offer a money-back guarantee with these principles for confrontation: "If you follow these biblical guidelines, the person who wronged you will repent, the sinful behavior will be decisively abandoned, and your relationship will be completely healed— or double your money back!" But that's completely unrealistic. Some people will go to their graves insisting that they were justified in lying, cheating, backstabbing, insulting, or otherwise mistreating people around them. Other people will add another offense to the list of their sins, bald-facedly denying what they have done. If your reproof is accepted, give praise to God, because the softening of a hardened heart is one of God's great wonders. But write your letter or go into your meeting confident that God *is* a God of miracles!

If your reproof strikes home in a heart softened and prepared by the Spirit, you may see a good deal of weeping. Don't let that embarrass you. Powerful feelings of sorrow and remorse are God-ordained instruments of lasting change. When the Bible depicts genuine repentance, it frequently describes it in terms of profound, overpowering emotions: "Wash your hands, you sinners, and purify your hearts, you double-minded. Grieve, mourn and wail. Change your laughter to mourning and your joy to gloom" (James 4:8-9).

The apostle Paul rejoiced when he learned of the painful emotions the Corinthian believers experienced when they received his rebuke, not because he was a sadist, but because their strong feelings were tokens of repentance: "I am happy, not because you were made sorry, but because your sorrow led you to repentance....See what this godly sorrow has produced in you: what earnestness, what eagerness to clear yourselves, what indignation, what alarm, what longing, what concern, what readiness to see justice done" (2 Corinthians 7:9,11).

What if the offender refuses to change after the confrontation? Even when the wrongdoer will not accept responsibility for his or her actions, some degree of reconciliation may be possible. Your relationship will be based on your willingness to forgive unconditionally and whatever limited changes in behavior you can negotiate with the wrongdoer.

In some situations the offender will insist, "I'll change! I'll change! I really mean it this time!" But certain addictive behaviors are notoriously difficult to change. One day the addict repents; the next day he relapses.

Many people are instantly delivered from an addiction. However, most substance abusers generally require a high degree of accountability and supervision to achieve permanent change. The biological craving for a substance can be so strong that professional assistance may be necessary. Similarly, a history of eating disorders, homosexuality and other sexual sins, or addiction to pornographic, violent, or occult literature and activities frequently call for close and extended personal counseling and discipleship if the person is to maintain steady spiritual growth.

If you are confronting someone who is extremely abusive to himself, you, or others, it is essential that you find someone to help you, such as a spiritually strong friend of the offender. If you use a professional counselor at any time, be sure he is a solid Christian and committed to putting you in touch with what God's Word commands, not simply committed to putting you in touch with your feelings!

If you choose family intervention for a serious offense, seek the guidance of an experienced Christian counselor or pastor. It is especially important to guard your heart in a serious situation. You must recognize that you may be tempted to nurture an unforgiving spirit. Your decisive action may open the door to your loved one's heart, but only the Holy Spirit can change his heart. If the other person simply isn't willing to change or grow, don't imagine that you can force the improvement. Leave that up to God and the offender. Place him in God's hands.

Speaking the truth in love is just that. It must be the truth, and love must rule. Depending on God for courage and believing God for results are essential. Don't be surprised if you sense that God is calling you to be an agent of change by "speaking the truth in love." Be confident that God will enable you to deal with the pain. You can be God's tool to bring about significant change and restoration in another person's life.

God is able to change any relationship for the better. With His help, reconciliation can be a reality. In the next chapter, we will discuss how.

_____14_____

The Realities of Reconciliation

A distraught young woman said to me, "I just can't forgive Greg. The thought of going back to him and trying to salvage our engagement leaves me physically sick. I just know I'll get hurt again. He really doesn't care, so I might as well face it and try to get on with my life."

Sally is doing what many offended people tend to do. She is making reconciliation a requirement for forgiveness. Sally is waffling on her decision to forgive her fiancé because she doesn't see any hope for their relationship to be restored. In her mind, if there is no reconciliation, there is no forgiveness.

Sally's response is not unusual, and it brings to the surface several important questions for people who are learning to love again after forgiving someone who offended them.

- Once you have forgiven a person, do you always seek to be reconciled?

- Forgiveness is commanded by God, but what about reconciliation?

- When you forgive your best friend for gossiping about you, do you open up the secrets of your heart to him again?

- If you forgive your associate for embezzling company funds, do you resume the original partnership?

- You have decided to forgive your ex-mate, but does that mean remarriage should be your goal?

Forgiveness paves the way for reconciliation, but the two are not the same. Forgiveness is radical surgery; reconciliation is the healing after the operation. Forgiveness is canceling the debt; reconciliation puts debt-free lives back together. Forgiveness is a decision to release; reconciliation is the effort to rejoin.

Our attitude toward reconciliation may reveal the sincerity of our forgiveness. If we say an absolute no to the possibility of resuming a relationship, we may be harboring resentment that the Holy Spirit wants to purge. When we forgive another person, we are entrusting that relationship to God. We must also be willing to consider His plans for the future of that relationship.

There are situations in which forgiveness will be naturally followed by steady progress toward reconciliation. In other relationships, we can truly forgive, and yet for some reason reconciliation will be impossible or unlikely.

Understanding the interplay between forgiveness and reconciliation requires a clear understanding of what the term reconciliation means.

What Is Reconciliation?

Here is a basic definition of reconciliation. As you can see, reconciliation has everything to do with our ability to love again:

Reconciliation is the pursuit of peace allowing for the restoration of a relationship according to the will of God.

If you ever want to love again in a pain-scarred relationship, you must become a peacemaker. Reconciliation begins with establishing a truce that will allow time for healing and the restoration of the relationship. What level of intimacy will you ultimately be able to achieve? That's something only God can determine.

In the Bible, reconciliation means to bring into agreement. It is typically used to describe relationships where obvious hostility has been replaced by peace or friendship. Most biblical uses are applied to our relationship with God. Because of sin we were enemies of God. The work of Jesus Christ on the cross not only provided forgiveness for our sins but reconciled us to God (Romans 5:9-11). When we place our faith in Christ, we cease being enemies and became His beloved children.

At least three Bible passages refer to reconciliation between people. Jesus said that if someone comes to the temple to offer a sacrifice and there realizes that a brother has something against him, he should first pursue reconciliation with his brother and then return to offer his sacrifice (Matthew 5:23-24). When an offense is keeping two people apart, they should seek to clear the air and live in harmony because peaceful, loving relationships honor God.

Ray and Diane are a delightful couple with a servant's heart and a real love for people. They were deeply hurt when another couple from their church began to avoid them. Ray and Diane couldn't figure out what had caused the rift in their relationship with these friends. This behavior went on for about a year, until finally Ray and Diane asked their friends what was wrong. They were shocked to find out that this couple had totally misinterpreted a conversation the four of them had at a church dinner.

Because Ray and Diane followed the biblical injunction to reconcile a wounded relationship, they were able to clear the air and resume their friendship. Their only regret was that they didn't do so sooner.

Reconciliation should also be pursued when we find ourselves being taken to court. Jesus said, "As you are going with your adversary to the magistrate, try hard to be reconciled to him on the way, or he may drag you off to the judge, and the judge turn you over to the officer, and the officer throw you into prison" (Luke 12:58). Once again, this is a situation where there has been a serious transgression. You may or may not be at fault—the passage doesn't say. Regardless, you should do whatever you can to reduce the tension and hostility.

A third passage that refers to reconciliation on the human level relates to marriage. A Christian husband or wife who separates from his/her spouse has one of two choices: remain unmarried or be reconciled to his/her mate (1 Corinthians 7:10-11). The marriage covenant demands that the relationship keep changing for the better no matter how bad it may be at a given time. Reconciliation in marriage is required as we will explain in the next chapter.

Peace Without Restoration

There are occasions when we can reach a "peace agreement" with an offender but should not attempt to reestablish the original relationship. As you consider these exceptions to reconciling a close relationship, be careful not to use them as excuses to avoid the other person altogether.

Don't restore a relationship that is sinful. I met with Tony, a muscle-bound maniac, after he destroyed the door to the apartment where he and his girlfriend, Kelly, lived. As we talked, he finally told me why he was so angry. Bottom line: He wanted out of his relationship with Kelly. But when he told her, she went berserk. Earlier in their relationship, Tony had made some big promises to Kelly to advance his cause sexually, and Kelly had given in to him. Now Tony wanted to pack his bags and leave, and Kelly wasn't about to let him go. Tony felt trapped, and so he exploded.

Eventually I met with both of them and explained how God viewed their relationship. I encouraged them to seek forgiveness from God and to extend forgiveness to each other. They did so. But then they began to discuss returning to their live-in arrangement. Should they resume their previous sinful level of intimacy? No way. We should not restore a relationship that is clearly outside the will of God (1 Corinthians 7:1-2; 1 Thessalonians 4:3-8). In cases like Tony and Kelly's, a gentle severing of the relationship is best.

Don't restore a relationship marked by physical or extreme emotional abuse. God doesn't expect you to immediately resume a relationship that places you in harm's way. A battered wife must approach her troubled husband cautiously and with outside help. Constraints must be in place and safety assured.

During a break in a marriage conference, a woman came up to me in tears. She said she was having a terrible time reconciling her relationship with her 82-year-old father, who was a patient in a psychiatric treatment center. This man was nothing short of vile. Whenever his daughter came to visit him, he would explode in a tirade of bitterness and profanity. The more she described her father, the more I suspected that he was severely oppressed by demons.

She was a bit shocked when I asked her, "Why do you subject yourself to such treatment?"

"He's my father!" she insisted.

I commended her for her love for him, but then I suggested that any attempts to meet with her father should be bathed in prayer, and that her husband should accompany her on her visits. If her father remained totally obnoxious, she should back off and try sending him some nice letters presenting the gospel.

When we have made an honest effort to reestablish a relationship and the other person is nothing short of dangerous, it's time to pull back (Proverbs 23:9).

Full reconciliation is impossible when the offender is still hostile. If the person you have forgiven won't drop his gloves of opposition, don't get in the ring with him. It takes two people to have a fight, and it also takes two to pull a relationship back together. If you're the only one interested, it won't happen.

Paul wrote, "If it is possible, as far as it depends on you, live at peace with everyone" (Romans 12:18). There will be times when you seek peace with someone who refuses to seek peace with you. The obligation rests with you to do everything you can to make the relationship right even when the offender maintains a hostile attitude toward you. When you have done your part, rest assured that you have done all that God expects of you.

Even when the offender is not interested in changing his behavior, you can still work toward a reasonable level of peace. Bill was so disgusted by his father's foul language, especially in front of his wife and children, that Bill finally confronted him. His father responded to the confrontation by blasting Bill with a stream of gutter talk. Bill realized that his father was not ready to change.

In weighing the offense and thinking about what he could do to keep peace in the relationship, Bill decided to continue their family visits. He leveled with the children about Grandpa's language, and they continued to see him and endure his periodic tirades. Bill sensed that the Lord wanted him to carefully guard his children while at the same time expressing unconditional love for his dad.

Don't restore a relationship that puts you in spiritual jeopardy. Biblical encouragement to reconcile should always be balanced by other admonitions to avoid spiritual danger. The Word of God warns us, "Bad company corrupts good character" (1 Corinthians 15:33). Paul told Timothy to avoid evil men and women who only *appear* to be godly (2 Timothy 3:1-5). And entering into intimate relationships with unbelievers is expressly forbidden by God (2 Corinthians 6:14).

If reconciliation places you or your family in spiritual jeopardy, don't do it. Doug's experience is a case in point. Doug had been a bartender for years and then became a Christian. He had wonderful opportunities to share his testimony with his barroom buddies. But rather than continue his close friendship with them and risk being tempted to return to that lifestyle, Doug decided to keep a polite distance, allowing him to reach out to his former buddies while protecting his own walk with the Lord.

When Should You
Initiate Reconciliation?

In most relationships where we have decided to forgive and confront an offender, reconciliation is a viable option. But initiating the process is a matter of critical timing. Here are some guidelines to help you know when to restore a relationship.

When the Spirit leads. The decision to attempt reconciliation must be God-inspired and Spirit-directed. While forgiveness is commanded in Scripture, reconciliation and the restoration of a relationship come under the leading of the Spirit of God.

We must remain open to this possibility no matter how great the offense was. The Holy Spirit knows what is happening in both hearts. He is the author of unity between Christians (Ephesians 4:3). He knows when the offender's heart has changed and when the time is right to move from simple peace to a greater level of closeness. Allow the Holy Spirit to counsel you through prayer and God's Word, and seek His timing and direction for restoring a damaged relationship.

When you are emotionally anchored. Before attempting reconciliation, it is absolutely essential that you are anchored to the Word of God. If your emotions are not founded solidly on the Word, you will be tempted to dredge up past offenses. If you haven't emotionally released your pain, you will be vulnerable not only to another offense but to a sinful, unforgiving spirit in your own heart.

If you find your heart fluttering with anxiety in the presence of the other person, go slowly. Don't try to immediately return to your former level of intimacy.

When you are genuinely concerned about the offender. As with confrontation, your heart must be right before pursuing reconciliation. Are you sincerely interested in the welfare of the one who hurt you? Have you been able to get your eyes off your own pain and see the hidden pain in that person's heart? Do you have a deep sense of the spiritual dynamics and possible demonic harassment that have created this difficult situation? Have you reached the point where you even hurt for the other person? Have you been able to pray for him and sincerely seek God's best for him? These are questions you must ask yourself before you proceed.

When you have the right attitude. Attempting reconciliation with the wrong attitude is dangerous. What is the correct attitude? You must be humble and gracious. Decide immediately that you will not be pushy. You can't force reconciliation on anyone. Aggressive attempts may only cause the offender to fall into a pattern of relating to you on a sinful level. Don't attempt to force intimacy, but instead be patient and exhibit the fruit of the Spirit (Galatians 5:22-23).

When the offender takes the initiative. "Barry wants to meet with me. Should I do it?" Sandy's concern was well-founded. Barry's history of abuse and infidelity rightfully caused her to question his motives. Was he looking for another chance to hurt her? Did he want money? Or was he really starting to come around?

Sandy needed to evaluate her ability to handle such a meeting. Could she bring her thoughts and emotions under the control of the Holy Spirit? Did she need someone else to go along with her for support?

When some form of reconciliation is initiated by an estranged friend or spouse, we should give it prayerful consideration. Don't be totally naive. As you walk through the open door, guard your heart and ask the Holy Spirit to guide and protect you and reveal how you should respond.

When death is imminent. Coming face-to-face with our own mortality often places relationships in proper perspective. When someone is on his deathbed, relationships with God, family, and others suddenly become very important. It's the last opportunity to reconcile a relationship before death severs it.

After I gave a message on heaven, a man came up to me and mumbled a few words about his father having just days to live. As I looked into his tear-filled eyes, he said, "We are both believers, but we have been at odds for years."

I advised him to go as quickly as possible to see his dad. Reconciliation was long overdue; petty differences should no longer stand in the way. It was time to say, "I love you, Dad, and I will see you soon."

How Should You Initiate Reconciliation?

Consider starting with a letter. The way you approach restoring a relationship is absolutely essential to your success. It doesn't take much to fan a small flame of anger or bitterness that still burns in a person's heart. A sharp word, a defiant gesture, or a harsh look is all it takes to resurrect the pain that's been buried. With these dynamics in mind, you might want to take your initial step toward reconciliation through a letter.

As with the letter of confrontation described in chapter 13, begin your letter of reconciliation with expressions of sincere love. Highlight some of the positive elements that once marked your relationship. Don't point the finger and say something accusatory. Yes, there are problems that need to be resolved. But your letter is intended to build a bridge. Discussing past offenses may come later. Finally, make it clear as you write that you want the relationship restored.

On the relatively rare occasions when my wife and I reach an emotional impasse, Teri will write down her feelings and explain how she has been hurt. Inevitably, as I read her letter, the Holy Spirit starts to work in my heart. He brings important passages to mind: "Husbands, love your wives" (Ephesians 5:25); "Husbands...be considerate as you live with your wives" (1 Peter 3:7). When I consider the letter openly and prayerfully, our oneness is soon restored.

Prepare for a personal encounter. There is no biblical timetable for restoring a relationship. It apparently took years before Paul and John Mark resumed their friendship (Colossians 4:10). We don't know if Euodia and Syntyche ever came to a point of agreement (Philippians 4:2). As you move from a simple cease-fire to a growing relationship, you must remain dependent on the Holy Spirit, the Divine Counselor.

Perhaps you have already initiated the process of reconciliation. You've written a letter asking for forgiveness for any wrong you committed and expressing your desire to tear down any emotional and relational walls between you. You feel that a personal meeting is the next step, but you're worried that a good start may be ruined once you encounter the individual and his faults in person. What can you do to protect yourself and your goal of reconciliation? Here are some biblical guidelines to help you make sure you are moving ahead in the right way and at the right time.

Seek agreement on mutual expectations. Do you know what lies behind most relationship problems? Unfulfilled expectations. When an individual doesn't communicate what he expects out of a relationship or has unrealistic expectations for his mate or friend, tension sets in and conflicts arise. In fact, most problems in churches are a by-product of poorly defined roles and responsibilities as well as unrealistic expectations.

One of the best ways to reconcile a relationship is to define and clarify mutual expectations. When Abraham and Lot determined it was best to go their separate ways, they entered into an amicable agreement for dividing land and possessions (Genesis 13:5-11).

The story of Abraham and Lot has a modern parallel in a couple I knew. Dick and Joan went through a terrible divorce. At that time they were not Christians. The battle over assets and custody of the children seemed endless.

Then something incredible happened. On a coast-to-coast airplane trip, Dick came to know Jesus Christ as his Savior. His life was dramatically changed. Soon after, Joan became a Christian at a women's Bible study.

The two new believers fell in love again and decided to get remarried. But before they did, they entered into a written agreement. Dick agreed to work and travel less, and Joan committed herself to being more supportive of Dick's efforts. Having clarified their expectations in this way, they continue to have a wonderful marriage.

Your reconciled relationship will have a better opportunity for health and growth if you verbalize your commitments to and expectations of each other.

Consider the providential circumstances. Our sovereign God directs relationships to accomplish His good and perfect will (Romans 8:28). As you look at the circumstances surrounding your relationships, recognize that God is in control. He may be encouraging some kind of deep reconciliation or He may arrange it so that reconciliation at a substantial level is impossible. Don't resist what God is trying to accomplish, but remain open and look at your specific situation to determine how you should respond.

Weigh the desires of your heart. The Bible tells us that if we delight ourselves in the Lord, He will give us the desires of our heart (Psalm 37:4-5). This truth assumes that our desires are in keeping with the will of God. If we are renewing our minds and are walking in close fellowship with the Savior, our feelings and desires will begin to reflect His will. Obviously, we must be careful in this regard. But it is safe to say that if you are walking in rich and vibrant fellowship with the Lord, your desire for reconciliation may well reveal His will for your relationship.

Open the door to love. Reconciliation is love's open door. The desire and determination to restore relationships says to God and to the offender, "I am willing to love again."

The greatest statement of love is found in 1 Corinthians 13:7: "[Love] always protects, always trusts, always hopes, always perseveres." Because love always protects, you will care about what happens to the other person. Because love always trusts, you will learn to become secure in your renewed relationship with him. Because love always hopes, you will see beyond the minor tensions and conflicts that inevitably arise even in the best relationships. And because love always perseveres, your loving concern for the other person will remain constant despite pressures that would drive you apart.

God's message of hope to you is that you can forgive and love again in relationships where you have been hurt. As you forgive the offender unconditionally and seek God's healing for your inner hurt, you are opening your heart to love again. As you lovingly confront the offender and remain open to reconciliation if the Holy Spirit so directs, you are building a bridge for both of you to love again.

The principles we have discussed in these chapters apply to all relationships. But the one relationship that will be the most dramatically impacted by these biblical truths is the marriage relationship. In the next chapter, we will explore some critical special applications for forgiving and loving again as husband and wife.

15

The Unique Demands of Marriage

*J*ennifer and Larry enjoyed a storybook high-school romance: the pretty cheerleader dating the celebrated captain of the football team. The magnetism between the two was mainly looks, popularity, and a heavy dose of hormones. When attending various school and church functions, they almost always struck a pose as the king and queen. On the surface they seemed to have it all together.

But behind the scenes the young couple fought constantly. Their arguments were intense and sometimes even violent. On several occasions Jennifer's parents talked to her about her love–hate relationship with Larry. Jennifer's response depended largely on where she was in the ongoing cycle of fighting and forgiving.

Every weekend, when Jennifer and Larry spent a great deal of time together, they eventually found themselves at odds with one another. By Sunday afternoon they had engaged in at least three or four skirmishes and had threatened to call off their relationship for good. But on Tuesday Larry was on the phone to Jennifer trying to smooth things out. By Thursday they made up, and on

Friday night they went out again, and the cycle started all over.

Jennifer's parents were concerned, but they decided not to take action to break them up, hoping their prayers and Jennifer's plans to go away to college would put an end to the painful and turbulent relationship.

When Jennifer and Larry went off to different colleges, no one expected their relationship to last beyond the first semester. Larry was playing football while Jennifer was busy with her pre-med studies. By Christmas of the couple's freshman year, Jennifer's parents thought their prayers were answered. Jennifer was showing interest in another young man at college and came home excited about the possibilities of the relationship. But after a few days home on Christmas break, she was seeing Larry again. Larry's mom, who had raised him alone, convinced Jennifer that her relationship with Larry was a match made in heaven.

Before Christmas break was over, Jennifer began to discuss transferring to the same college Larry attended. Although her parents voiced strong opposition, Jennifer merely grew closer to Larry. They sensed they were losing their daughter.

The romance that started in high school endured through college. Even though Jennifer had started to pull away from her parents, they were still able to discern that the couple's routine of weekend break-up and mid-week make-up was continuing.

During Christmas break of their senior year, Larry and Jennifer announced their marriage plans. Jennifer's parents were perplexed, especially when they saw how happy Jennifer seemed to be. There was something about a Christmas engagement that made it all seem right.

The following year was packed with preparations for graduation and, a month later, the wedding. The ceremony was filled with splendor and beauty, epitomizing what God intends for a marriage. Larry told his friends that he was marrying his childhood sweetheart and, in a way, he was. But what he failed to realize was that when a relationship moves from courtship to marriage it undergoes dramatic changes.

Several years and two children later, Larry called me for an appointment. His first words were, "Jennifer and I fight all the time. It just keeps getting worse. I'm at the point where I really need some space. I need to move out. What do you think?"

When I asked him what was happening between them, Larry described a scenario found in so many marriages. Jennifer was a young mother under intense pressure caring for a toddler and a little baby. Larry was under stress at work. When he came home he just wanted time to be alone. He felt content if he could read his newspaper or watch television and then go to bed. Whenever Jennifer asked him to do something, he would explode. Once set off, his temper raged for days like an uncontrollable forest fire.

I soon came to realize that Larry and Jennifer entered marriage assuming that wedding bells and "I do's" would solve all their problems. Instead, they found marriage intensifying their conflicts. What they had done was to bring their relationship problems into a new setting while adding the greater demands and pressures of marriage.

God created the marriage relationship to be unique in human experience. There is no other relationship so demanding yet so potentially rewarding. Marriage requires us to live with another person in the closest union known to mankind. Such intimacy can be intimidating. We are compelled to reveal our true selves, often prompting a fear of rejection. Once we move beyond our fears of transparency, we discover that there is no relationship more wonderful. It is in this divine union that we have our greatest opportunities to forgive and love again.

Choosing to Forgive in Marriage

Forgive repeated offenses. When Jesus mentioned forgiving someone "seventy times seven," He must have had marriage in mind. When two people live together, certain offenses will be repeated—count on it! I know you have a ready list of things your mate does that drive you to the edge of insanity (and he or she has a list for you!). You each have certain annoying habit patterns that seem to persist no matter what you say or do. It is important to recognize that forgiving each other's repeated offenses and praying together for growth and change is essential to the marriage relationship.

Love and forgiveness find their greatest test and enjoy their greatest fulfillment in marriage. Do you remember the story of the repentant prostitute who bathed Jesus' feet with her tears and dried them with her hair (Luke 7:36-50)? After she had exhibited such respect and love for the Master, He told a story about two men who owed money to a lender. One owed 500 denarii; the other just 50. Neither had the ability to pay the debt, so the lender graciously canceled both debts. Then Jesus posed the question, "Which man will love the lender more?" The obvious answer was the man who was forgiven more loved more.

Forgiveness generates love in its fullest form. When we are forgiven much, we love much. Although Jesus had in mind our loving response to God's forgiveness, the principle holds true on the human level. In marriage, generous forgiveness for repeated offenses generates deep and abiding love. I have watched a number of repentant adulterers who have been forgiven by their mates respond with great loyalty and devotion.

A good friend of mine fell into the terrible trap of alcoholism. It finally brought him to his knees, and he turned to several friends for help, including me. This man's honesty and courage in facing his problem challenged me in my walk with the Savior. But what intrigued me even more was his wife's loving support and willingness to forgive. She stood with him even during his drunken stupors and sleepless nights.

One day my friend tried to summarize all his wife had done to tolerate and forgive him. With tears streaming down his face, he said, "I don't know how she could love me the way she has. I owe her my life." Now, after a number of years of sobriety, this man's love for his wife is unmatched.

Keep short accounts. Every Christian couple ought to have Ephesians 4:26 on a plaque in bold letters above their bed: "Do not let the sun go down while you are still angry." Perhaps you would prefer to post a paraphrased version: "Forgive your mate or stay up late!" The message is clear: Don't go to sleep until you clean up anything that has littered your relationship during the day.

The warning to keep short accounts is given so we don't "give the devil a foothold" (v. 27). How can the devil get a foothold in your marriage? Often very subtly. At dinner your husband makes a remark that irks you. You say nothing because the children are there. You put off talking about it until later, and before you know it you are both heading for bed.

The next thing you know, your husband is making amorous advances. You're still angry about what he said at dinner, but you know he won't even remember it. He senses your reluctance and it bothers him, but he refuses to say anything. He simply rolls over and falls asleep. Meanwhile, your adrenaline flows, fueled by your anger, and keeps you awake. You struggle to get to sleep and find that your anger only grows every time you hear him snore.

The next day you both wake up feeling a bit empty. You're not really sure why. Your unresolved anger has become a foothold for the great destroyer of families. Every time you fail to deal with offenses, you allow Satan to get a firmer grip. The better his grip, the easier it is for him to push you apart.

That's why the Bible commands us to forgive promptly—especially before the day ends. We must keep short accounts or pay an incredible price for our stubbornness. Forgive daily.

Strive for marital oneness. Marriage is unlike any other relationship. Only in marriage are two persons forged into a physical, emotional, and spiritual oneness. Lack of forgiveness strains and interrupts this oneness at every level. Unresolved offenses interrupt your physical oneness. You turn away from each other in bed, or one of you stomps away to sleep on the couch. Unforgiveness disrupts emotional unity; you stop talking with each other. Worst of all, unforgiveness severs your spiritual oneness. You stop praying and reading the Bible together or you continue to have devotions as hypocrites, pretending everything is okay between you.

If there is unforgiveness in your marriage, you might as well forget worshiping together. Jesus warned us not to bring a gift to the altar if there is something between us and a loved one (Matthew 5:23-24). Paul instructs us to examine ourselves before celebrating the Lord's table (1 Corinthians 11:27-29). This self-examination includes our horizontal relationships, especially the relationship of marriage. If your marriage is in disorder, your capacity to develop spiritually is in danger.

A clear revelation of this truth is found in 1 Peter 3:7. While the first six verses of this chapter reveal ways by which a godly woman can win her husband to the Lord, verse 7 is suddenly directed to the husband: "Husbands, in the same way be considerate as you live with your wives, and treat them with respect as the weaker partner and as heirs with you of the gracious gift of life, so that nothing will hinder your prayers."

A husband is to understand the way God made his wife and treat her considerately because she shares in the gracious gift of eternal life and is a fellow heir of the things of God. What happens if he fails to do this? His prayers will be hindered. If a husband doesn't treat his wife properly, he may not be praying at all or his prayers will be turned away from the throne of heaven.

Oneness in marriage depends on each partner seeking and extending forgiveness to the other, *continually* restoring their unique partnership. The act of forgiveness is a wonderful way to experience the grace of God while extending to each other what God has graciously extended to you.

Learning to Love Again in Marriage

Forgiveness is required in all our relationships, but confrontation and reconciliation are dependent on the circumstances and the Holy Spirit's leading. Marriage is the exception. The God-ordained oneness of the marriage relationship requires that husbands and wives not only forgive each other's offenses but follow through with the steps necessary to assure reconciliation.

When you were first married, your emotions ran high. There was nothing more exhilarating than your wedding day, and it was capped off by a wonderful honeymoon. Romance, passion, and celebration escorted you as you paraded into the marriage covenant. You were sure nothing could come between you and your spouse because you both were so deeply in love. But once you settled in, your emotions changed. Romance was occasionally overcome by rage and passion by pain.

We have already considered the biblical admonition to guard our hearts as we forgive others and pursue emotional healing. The need to guard our hearts is especially acute in the marriage relationship, because our expectations for marriage make us so vulnerable. We expected the romance to continue at a fever pitch, but it hasn't. We expected the passion to always be there, but it comes and goes. If we fail to forgive and love again in marriage, we will find our relationship becoming emotionally bankrupt. Marriage can survive a great deal of external stress, but few marriages survive emotional death. Forgiveness, reconciliation, and striving after oneness are essential to maintaining a healthy emotional relationship.

Confront each other gently and lovingly. Those who know my wife and recognize her sweet and gentle spirit often assume that I pretty much get my way and that Teri always responds to me with a servant's heart. She certainly has a servant's heart and a loving spirit, but that doesn't mean she lets me get away with something that needs to be corrected.

Teri has confronted me in love on a number of occasions, and she doesn't mince words. She has confronted me over my struggle to maintain my temper. She has confronted me on things I have done to offend her and our children. While I never enjoy being confronted with my delinquency, Teri's willingness to speak the truth in love has been a source of great blessing to me. In fact, it's her sweet and gentle spirit that makes her confronting words all the more difficult to ignore. She is not in the habit of preaching at me, so when she speaks I know I need to listen.

Marriage demands an accountability relationship before each other and God. The willingness to confront each other can be our first line of defense against moving away from God. The husband who sees his wife ignoring spiritual disciplines is the one who needs to encourage her to change. The wife who sees her husband exasperating the children is the one who needs to take him aside and warn him.

You must confront each other sensitively and with the right attitude, but you must speak when a wrong needs to be addressed. If you truly love your mate, don't remain silent while he or she lives a pattern that is self-destructive or harmful to you, your family, or the cause of Christ.

Reconciliation is required. In other relationships it is possible to allow a gap of time between forgiveness and reconciliation. There are natural intervals of separation built into most relationships. These cushions of time afford us the opportunity to bring our emotions under control and spend extended time absorbing the truth of God's Word before we consider making a move toward reconciliation.

But in marriage we have a different requirement. Marriage involves living together continually. In fact, in 1 Corinthians 7:1-5 we are instructed to live together and share physical oneness together on a regular basis to avoid temptation, only refraining from togetherness for short time periods (and then only for prayer!). Because marriage is not a casual relationship, we must do everything we can to be at peace with each other and cultivate a relationship that reflects the kind of loving, unbreakable union that exists between Christ and His church.

In marriage, reconciliation means being continually committed to closeness, oneness, and divine partnership. There may be times when you want some personal space to deal with extremely intense conflicts between you. In extreme cases, it may be appropriate to occasionally spend some time apart under the guidance of a Holy Spirit-directed counselor. But God's command to married couples is to be reconciled one to another. Do whatever it takes to make your relationship what God wants it to be. Follow His truth, *not your emotions*, concerning your role in the marriage relationship.

Teach and model forgiveness before your children. If your marriage has been blessed with children, you realize the kind of world in which they are growing up. Hostilities abound, and your kids will experience significant relational hurts in the years ahead. One of the best gifts you can give your children is the forgiving spirit you exemplify and teach.

You have several opportunities to encourage forgiveness every day. Use sibling rivalry to help your children learn what it means not to keep a record of wrongs done. Require that they ask for and extend forgiveness. They may do so through clenched teeth, but at least they will know what they should do in conflict situations.

Applying these truths in the midst of your children's skirmishes is essential, but its impact is nominal compared to your model of forgiveness as a couple. Your children need to see that you love each other enough to always forgive. As you forgive each other, you provide your children much-needed security. Your willingness to forgive your mate will always be a great stabilizer in your home.

The marriage relationship is unique, and so is the application of forgiveness, confrontation, and reconciliation within marriage. Forgiveness will be tested to the limits between husband and wife. Confrontation will need to be approached with the utmost of care. And reconciliation must be sought and achieved in the fullest measure. Are you willing to give it a try? Go ahead. Do what the Bible says: Trust God and see Him work.

We close with a prayer for your marriage that was written by the late Dr. Louis H. Evans. His wife graciously granted us permission to share it with you.

O God of Love, Thou hast established marriage for the welfare and happiness of mankind. Thine was the plan, and only with Thee can we work it out with joy. Thou has said, "It is not good for man to be alone. I will make a help meet for him." Now our joys are doubled since the happiness of one is the happiness of the other. Our burdens now are halved when we share them, we divide the load.

Bless this husband. Bless him as provider of nourishment and raiment and sustain him in all the exactions and pressures of his battle for bread. May his strength be her protection, his character be her boast and her pride, and may he so live that she will find in him the haven for which the heart of woman truly longs.

Bless this loving wife. Give her tenderness that will make her great, a deep sense of understanding and a great faith in Thee. Give her that inner beauty of soul that never fades, that eternal youth that is found in holding fast the things that never age.

Teach them that marriage is not living merely for each other; it is two uniting and joining hands to serve Thee. Give them a great spiritual purpose in life. May they seek first the kingdom of God and His righteousness, and the other things shall be added unto them.

May they not expect that perfection of each other that belongs alone to Thee. May they minimize each other's weaknesses, be swift to praise and magnify each other's points of comeliness and strength, and see each other through a lover's kind and patient eyes.

Now make such assignments to them on the scroll of Thy will as will bless them and develop their characters as they walk together. Give them enough tears to keep them tender, enough hurts to keep them humane, enough of failure to keep their hands clenched tightly in Thine, and enough success to make them sure they walk with God.

May they never take each other's love for granted, but always experience that breathless wonder that exclaims, "Out of all this world you have chosen me."

When life is done and the sun is setting, may they be found then as now hand in hand, still thanking God for each other. May they serve Thee happily, faithfully, together, until at last one shall lay the other into the arms of God.

This we ask through Jesus Christ, great lover of our souls. Amen.

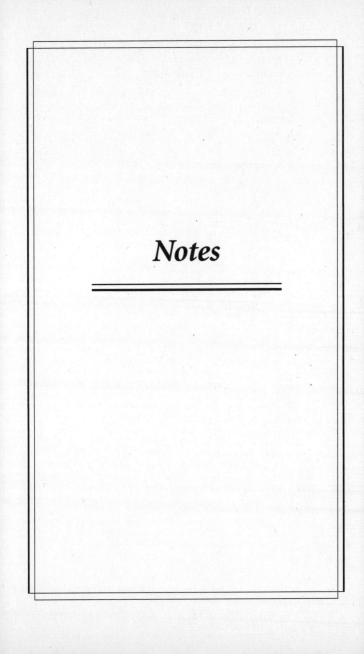

Notes

_____Notes_____

Chapter 3—Accept No Substitutes

1. Susan Forward, *Toxic Parents* (New York: Bantam Books, 1989).
2. David Augsburger, *Caring Enough to Forgive* (Ventura, CA: Regal Books, 1981).
3. Maureen Rank, *Dealing with the Dad of Your Past* (Minneapolis: Bethany House, 1990), p. 84.

Chapter 4—The Dangers of Unforgiveness

1. Neil T. Anderson, *The Bondage Breaker* (Eugene, OR: Harvest House Publishers, 1990), p. 194.
2. Charles R. Swindoll, *Stress Fractures* (Portland, OR: Multnomah Press, 1990), pp. 206-207.
3. Malcolm Boyd, "Familial Mixed Blessings," *Modern Maturity* (April–May, 1991), p. 78.

Chapter 5—The Model of True Forgiveness

1. There is no particular "chapter and verse" from which these word pictures are derived. However, these various "word picture" meanings come from no less than 88 different usages of the word "forgiveness" in the Bible. In the Hebrew and Greek languages used in Bible times, the term "release" is the best one-word definition of the word "forgiveness."

   Arndt, William F. and F. Wilbur Gingrich, *A Greek-English Lexicon of the New Testament* (Chicago: University of Chicago Press, 1957).

   Kittel, Gerhard and Gerhard Friedrich, *Theological Dictionary of the New Testament*, 9 vols. (Grand Rapids, MI: William B. Eerdmans Publishing Co., 1974).

Harris, R. Laird and Gleason L. Archer Jr., and Waltke, Bruce K., *Theological Word Book of the Old Testament*, 2 vols. (Chicago: Moody Press, 1980).

Brown, Colin, ed., *The New International Dictionary of New Testament Theology* (Grand Rapids, MI: Zondervan Publishing House, 1975).

Chapter 7—Where Do You Go to Forgive?

1. Corrie ten Boom, *Tramp for the Lord* (Fort Washington, PA: Christian Literature Crusade, Inc., and Old Tappan, NJ: Fleming H. Revell Company, 1974), pp. 182-183.

Chapter 8—Let Yourself Off the Hook

1. Neil T. Anderson, *Victory over the Darkness* (Ventura, CA: Regal Books, 1990), adapted from pp. 45-47.

Chapter 9—Do You Need to Forgive God?

1. Jerry Bridges, *Trusting God Even When Life Hurts* (Colorado Springs, CO: NavPress, 1988), p. 25.
2. Leith C. Anderson, *Making Happiness Happen* (Wheaton, IL: Victor Books, 1987), pp. 96-99.
3. Charles R. Swindoll, *Growing Strong in the Seasons of Life* (Portland, OR: Multnomah Press, 1983), adapted from p. 92.

Chapter 10—Maintaining a Forgiving Heart

1. Merrill F. Unger, *What Demons Can Do to Saints* (Chicago: Moody Press, 1991), p. 56.
2. Expanded translation following the thought of R.C.H. Lenski, *The Interpretation of St. Paul's First and Second Epistles to the Corinthians* (Minneapolis, MN: Augsburg Publishing House, 1937), pp. 1195-1210.

Other Great
Harvest House Books

Don't Give In...God Wants You to Win!
Thelma Wells

Is stress, indecision, heartache, or fear zapping your energy? Popular speaker and author Thelma Wells says life doesn't have to be that way! Opening her heart and God's Word, she reveals how God taught her to stand tall to win against discouragement and oppression by putting on God's armor. You'll discover:

- what spiritual warfare is
- who you're fighting
- what you're accomplishing

Thelma's contagious energy and enthusiasm invites you to tackle life with a "can do" attitude. You'll find great ways to dress for successful spiritual battle by:

- fixing your hair
  (putting on the helmet of salvation in Jesus for safety)
- padding your heart
  (donning the breastplate of righteousness to confront evil)
- putting on your stomping shoes
  (stepping out in faith against the devil)

No human wins every fight, so Thelma encourages you to call on Jesus when you get tired. He wants you to win, and He actively participates with you to ensure victory.

The Book of Bible Promises
Ron Rhodes

Hundreds of Bible promises are waiting for you. Let Bible scholar and author Ron Rhodes show you how to recognize what is and what is not a promise of God and give you a quick and easy way to look them up in Scripture. Develop a deeper faith while discovering what you've always wanted to know about

- God's faithfulness, goodness, and love
- fear, doubt, and your other emotions
- temptations, trials, and life's challenges

Understanding God's promises strengthens your relationship with Him and gives you the ability to walk confidently into the wonderful future He has for you.

Hot Topics for Couples
Steve and Annie Chapman

Whether you are newlyweds or seasoned partners, *Hot Topics for Couples* can help. What are the hot-button issues every couple struggles with? Drawing on 30-plus years of marriage, biblical wisdom, and survey responses, Steve and Annie reveal the difficult areas and offer practical ways to navigate them. You'll discover straightforward advice and conversation starters on topics that include...

- gender differences in sexuality
- "honey dos" and "honey don'ts" for both spouses
- leading, following, and making it work
- money, money, money
- the ups and downs of change

As an added bonus, interactive questions will help you and your mate develop an even stronger relationship. You can build a dynamic marriage based on love, cooperation, and flexibility that will become more joyful and satisfying every year!

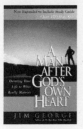

A Man After God's Own Heart

Jim George

Become a man who makes a lasting difference. Wouldn't you like to have a significant and lasting impact on the world around you?

God knows what it really takes for you to experience the satisfaction that comes from living a life of purpose. In *A Man After God's Own Heart,* author Jim George shares God's perfect design for how you can become a man who makes a real difference—in *all* the key areas of your life:

Your marriage—what it means to love, lead, and protect your wife

Your children—the keys to training up your children and shaping their hearts

Your work—modeling integrity and diligence in the workplace

Your church—discovering how and where God can use you best

Your witness—letting the world see God in your life and words

Gain the strength and wisdom that comes from pursuing God by becoming a man after God's own heart.